In The Power of a Plan, *David Stone presents an interesting and informative overview of the many elements embodied in a comprehensive financial plan. A Certified Financial Planner™ professional with over twenty years' experience, David describes real-life events and the benefits when proper planning was in place, as well as the consequences when it wasn't. Whether you're just starting out or have already accumulated substantial wealth,* The Power of a Plan *will help you understand the benefit of having your own "Personal CFO."*

Richard P. Rojeck, CFP®
Former chairman of the CFP® Board of Standards

the
POWER
of a PLAN

the
POWER
of a PLAN

How a Personal CFO Can Help

Business Owners & Professionals Prosper

DAVID E. STONE

Published by Advantage, Charleston, South Carolina.
Member of Advantage Media Group.

ADVANTAGE is a registered trademark and the Advantage colophon is a trademark of Advantage Media Group, Inc.

Printed in the United States of America.

ISBN: 978-1-59932-721-1
LCCN: 2016944066

Cover design by Matt Morse.

This publication is designed to provide accurate and authoritative information in regard to the subject matter covered. It is sold with the understanding that the publisher is not engaged in rendering legal, accounting, or other professional services. If legal advice or other expert assistance is required, the services of a competent professional person should be sought.

 Advantage Media Group is proud to be a part of the Tree Neutral® program. Tree Neutral offsets the number of trees consumed in the production and printing of this book by taking proactive steps such as planting trees in direct proportion to the number of trees used to print books. To learn more about Tree Neutral, please visit **www.treeneutral.com.**

Advantage Media Group is a publisher of business, self-improvement, and professional development books and online learning. We help entrepreneurs, business leaders, and professionals share their Stories, Passion, and Knowledge to help others Learn & Grow. Do you have a manuscript or book idea that you would like us to consider for publishing? Please visit **advantagefamily.com** or call **1.866.775.1696.**

This book is designed for informational purposes only, and should not be considered a recommendation or investment advice in any way. Any financial decisions you make should be made based on your current financial situation and in consultation with your tax and financial professionals. This book is not intended to be considered tax or legal advice, and should be considered the opinions of the author solely at the time of publication. This material does not represent the views or opinions of Lincoln Financial Group or its affiliates. Images and references to Lincoln Financial, Sagemark Consulting and the Resource Group are used with permission.

This book is dedicated to Ted Santon and Nick Horn, retired regional CEOs with Lincoln Financial Advisors, who took a chance on a young, eager MBA graduate from Northern California in 1992. Their dedication to the "Serve First" philosophy and commitment to the comprehensive financial-planning process continues to provide a North Star to me as a financial professional as my staff and I strive to provide five-star service to my clients so they will be able to experience the Power of a Plan.

TABLE OF CONTENTS

FOREWORD

In 1992, my friend David Stone had a dream—or maybe more of a nightmare, as he describes it. He told me he was at a funeral in the San Francisco Bay Area, where I lived at the time. It wasn't just any funeral, it was *my* funeral! I had left behind my wife, April, and our three small children under the age of six. This dream had really shaken David.

You see, David and I had been best friends since we were about three years old. We grew up in the same community in Northern California; attended the same elementary, junior high, and high schools; and attended the same church. We hung out after school virtually every day. David and I played on the high school football team together and were on the high school track team together. We were pretty much inseparable. We were even college roommates at Brigham Young University before we both left to serve missions for our church from 1983 to 1985. In fact, we even received our mission call letters on the same day in July 1983, me to North Carolina and David to South Africa. When we returned to California, we both headed back to Provo, Utah, to finish college, and yes, we were roommates again until I met my future wife, and a year later David met his bride. (Side note: we are both still married to those same amazing women almost thirty years later.) We were in each other's weddings. David says that I was his honorary best man but officially chose his younger brother, and I officially chose my older brother but thought of David as an extra best man, too.

After we were both married and started having kids, we both continued with our education and graduated from college. I went into the technology industry, and David went into finance. In fact, April and I became one of David's first financial-planning clients shortly after he graduated from MBA school. It was during this first financial-planning experience that David told me about his dream/nightmare. As David describes it, he found himself in the dream attending my funeral. It freaked him out. Here he was at my funeral, and he said that everyone, I mean *everyone*, was coming up to him and expressing sorrow for the loss of his best friend, and then everyone asked David the same question. Over and over, again and again, every one of our friends from high school, college, our church, our families asked David the same question: "April and the kids are going to be okay, *right*!?"

David had this dream around the time he was in the middle of designing our first financial plan. He had determined that there was a substantial need for life insurance, and the dream brought home his desire to make sure he was doing the right thing professionally for me and my family. That says a lot about him. So dedicated to his work that even his subconscious mind was working to help me do what I needed to do for my family through my plan. I took his advice and did the things that he recommended to help my family get our financial-planning foundation organized. It has been an ongoing process over the years. You see, doing financial planning on a comprehensive basis is not a one-time event; it is a process and an ongoing process at that. And the great news is that I am okay. I didn't die! *And* April and the kids (now six of them, mostly adults with children of their own) are doing just fine, thanks in part to a guy I often refer to as my personal CFO. You see, over the many years that have passed, David and his associates have been there for the Feller family and have helped play a part in some amazing things that have helped us to hang on and grow our small business, which we started in our basement. That business has now grown into a very successful business enterprise.

I hope you will find this book helpful as you try to figure out how best to build and protect your personal wealth. One thing is for sure, David Stone truly believes in the Power of a Plan. As a man of integrity, loyalty, and professionalism, he has also helped us see the value in the Power of a Plan as well. Hopefully you will take advantage of the concepts in this book to help you get your financial house in order. Enjoy!

KIRK M. FELLER
President & CEO

 Winner of "CES Innovations Award"
#436 of the Inc. 500 "Fastest Growing Companies in America"
Winner of "International Service Excellence Award" by CSIA

ACKNOWLEDGMENTS

Writing a book is a huge undertaking, and I cannot begin to express the gratitude I have for so many individuals who have impacted my life personally and professionally throughout this process. Each has made significant contributions to this process, my professional career, or both. I thank them for making such an impact on me.

To my wife, Sabrina, who made me laugh when she commented after reading the draft of the first chapter, "The book is way more interesting than I thought it was going to be." Sabrina has been so supportive throughout my professional career. I never could have taken on this project without my best friend keeping me grounded and focused on the things that are most important. She truly is my best friend and the best spouse anyone could ask for. I am the luckiest man in the world because of her.

To my children, Katelyn, Chandler, Carli, Summer, and Colton; my son-in-law, Marcus; and my grandchildren Georgia and Remington, for showing me love. I appreciate their support and motivation to follow my dreams and their giving me soccer teams to coach and Boy Scout troops to serve. They are such a joy to be around and make life as their father a great blessing.

To my mother, Patricia, and my father, Ronald V. "Bud," who raised me to understand the importance of trust, integrity, and service. Their examples of service continue to inspire in me a great desire to serve others in my church and community, both personally and professionally. The fact that my parents, being successful business owners themselves, waited three years before they actually hired me back in 1995 motivated me to build a practice that would truly provide the type of quality professional advice that business owners and professionals desired. (Since Stone Consulting Group remains in business after all these years, I believe we must be doing something right.)

To my clients, who have provided and continue to provide my professional associates and me the opportunity to give advice and access to the financial marketplace. You help me to fulfill a saying my grandmother used to quote often while I was growing up: "It is better to be trusted than to be loved." Thank you for the trust that you have placed in me and the opportunity to educate and serve you. Providing service focused on your hopes and dreams brings enormous professional satisfaction to me and everyone on my team.

To the former employees and financial-planning associates who have been a part of Stone Consulting Group over the years. Your dedication to clients, service, and professionalism, along with your insight and feedback, has meant a great deal to me and has helped me to grow personally and professionally. I could not have done this alone.

To Leslie Eriksson, former employee of Stone Consulting Group, thank you for coming up with the "Power of a Plan" as a creative way to communicate what is special about our planning-focused relationship with our clients.

To Kerri Self and Dana Vega, whose patience and professionalism have been amazing while I have been putting much of my energy into writing this book. Your encouragement as each of you assisted with proofreading the multiple drafts of this book has been amazing. I am thankful to you for keeping the business running smoothly while I was somewhat preoccupied with putting *The Power of a Plan* into words.

To Tom Christensen, regional director of planning with Lincoln Financial Advisors in San Ramon, California, and his predecessors over the past twenty-plus years, who have provided me with the plan manufacturing and collaboration needed to help my clients experience the Power of a Plan. His professionalism and creativity have been excellent as we work together to create hundreds of customized business and financial plans for our clients. As we work together and collaborate on our clients' comprehensive financial and business plans, it feels like 1 + 1 = 3!

To the members of The Resource Group (TRG) and its current board of directors, for the support I received as chairman of the board. The professional collaboration since 2002 has been an invaluable part of learning and understanding unique and alternative strategies to benefit my clients. To Larry Phillips, former CEO of TRG, and Hilary Dietz, executive director of TRG, for their amazing support to me personally while I served on committees and as chairman. To Anne Machesky, current chairman, and Stu Viets, former chairman, for their leadership and teamwork on the TRG executive committee.

To Ted Santon, Nick Horn, Aaron Jeung, Briggs Matsko, Celeste Gurule, John Mullen, Bob Waldron, Chris McClure, Michael Strohl, Bill Fortner, Madelyn Dreyer, Lauren Farasati, and the rest of the individual managers and trainers throughout my career at Lincoln Financial Advisors, who have supported me and trained me on the technical aspects of comprehensive financial planning and have given me a deep understanding of the planning process.

To Russ Jones, Doug Richmond, and Bill Wright, the executive directors and managers of Sagemark Consulting Private Wealth Services, who have provided me with advanced education and processes to deliver an exceptional client experience. To Amy Leavitt, who as a successful practitioner helped provide me with a long-term vision for Stone Consulting Group. I am grateful to all of them and for their ability to teach me the appropriate way to clearly communicate the merits of financial and business owner planning to our prospective and existing clientele. The comprehensive financial-planning process with Lincoln Financial Advisors and Sagemark Consulting helped us shape our planning processes at Stone Consulting Group.

And finally, to my editor, Howard Goldberg, whose decades of professional experience as an editor, manager, and journalist have been extremely important to me as a first-time author.

As I worked to provide you, the reader, an opportunity to learn and benefit from the concepts of my years of experience in the financial services industry, my greatest desire was for you to personally experience the Power of a Plan. I also thank the rest of the team at my publisher, Advantage Media, for their encouragement, support, and patience as we worked to meet the deadlines and provide you an interesting and helpful book.

AUTHOR'S NOTE

The privacy of my clients and of other families dealing with the personal issues discussed in this book are of the utmost importance to me. For this reason, names and some other identifying details of several people whose stories are contained in these pages have been changed to protect their identity. In addition, the examples provided for this book are specific to those individuals and families and may not necessarily represent the experiences of all clients.

HONEST ABE AND THE POWER OF A PLAN

In 1905, Robert Todd Lincoln, the son of Abraham Lincoln, was approached by a group of investors from Indiana. These gentlemen, one of whom was an attorney by the name of Arthur Hall, had a desire to create a company named after Abraham Lincoln. In fact, they were interested in not only using his name but also using his likeness on their letterhead. They had a desire to use a photo of Honest Abe for the public to connect President Lincoln and his reputation as a man of integrity to the financial services that they would provide. Robert Todd Lincoln responded to their request by sending the letter aside on August 3, 1905.

In addition to approving the name of the company and his father's likeness

to be used on the company letterhead, Robert Todd Lincoln attached an original photo of the former president. This photo was one that Robert regarded as a "very good photograph of him." Rumor has it that this photo was used as a reference by the Federal Reserve when adding President Lincoln's likeness to the five-dollar bill in the 1920s.

After receiving approval from the Lincoln family, Arthur Hall and the rest of the original investors started Lincoln National Life Insurance Company. Over the next century, the company evolved into what is known today as Lincoln Financial Group, a Fortune 500 company that trades as Lincoln National Corp., ticker LNC, on the New York Stock Exchange.

What does Abraham Lincoln have to do with financial planning or having a Personal CFO? After graduating with a BS in business management from the Marriott School of Management at BYU in 1988 and a master's degree in business administration (MBA) from California State University, Sacramento in 1992, I was introduced to Lincoln. Of course, I mean Lincoln the company. In that interview, I was told about a unique concept that wasn't very common at that time—professional consulting that included providing financial advice to individuals and business owners through a comprehensive analysis called financial planning.

WHAT IS FINANCIAL PLANNING?

After interviewing with fifteen different financial companies, from banks to wire houses to insurance companies to consulting firms, I determined that this "financial-planning" idea sounded perfect based on my education and life experience. This would become the career I would build over the next two decades and beyond. As I continued my research, I found that the definition of "financial planning" differed among companies. Some companies defined it exclusively as investment management. Some focused on the importance of insurance products and why they were a critical part of financial planning. Others looked at the benefits of tax planning or estate planning as the most important focus of their business. It intrigued me that companies defined it in so many different ways, and I recognized the merits in all of the different companies' areas of focus.

Separately, each provided benefits to the consumer, but it seemed like they all needed to be interconnected in some way. For example, tax planning was impacted by investment decisions, and the legal aspects of estate planning and asset protection were also impacted by choices made regarding life insurance ownership and beneficiaries as well as choices regarding real estate or other investments.

After some research, I found that there was a financial-planning organization called the CFP® Board of Standards. CFP® stands for Certified Financial Planner™. This group, founded in 1985, had a definition of financial planning that was to bring all of these different areas of expertise into one comprehensive plan to benefit the consumer. Affiliating with a company that thought everything should be coordinated between advisors to maximize the possibility for success seemed to me like the best choice. Of the fifteen different companies I interviewed with, there was only one, at the time, that explained their definition of financial planning to me like what I read from the CFP® Board of Standards.

In 1992, I chose to accept an offer from what is now known as Lincoln Financial Advisors, a subsidiary company of the organization that Arthur Hall and a handful of other businessmen in Indiana started in 1905. The main reason I decided to join this company was that they educated me about the importance of incorporating nearly every aspect of financial planning and the importance of coordinating that effort with the client's other legal and tax professionals. I was also impressed with how important it was to focus on doing whatever was in the best interest of the client and not the planner or the company.

Eventually, I was taught the "Serve First" philosophy (see Appendix B) and "The Creed" (see Appendix C) that state that a financial advisor should be focused on the client's needs by serving them first, last, and always. This had been a foundation of Lincoln's financial planning group since Stuart Smith, a legendary financial advisor and manager of a company that would later merge with Lincoln, created it in the 1940s. In 2005, I received what's called the Stuart Smith Award from the Lincoln Financial Advisors Pacific Regional Planning Group. The award is given to the advisor in Northern California, Oregon, Washington, or Alaska whose business practices most closely represent the Serve First philosophy. The honor caught me completely off guard but helped me and my staff recognize that, even inside of Lincoln, our planning philosophy was appreciated.

After all these years, Stone Consulting Group still uses Lincoln Financial Advisors as our Registered Investment Advisory firm in addition to acting as our broker-dealer. With Stone Consulting Group, our clients get the personal attention of a boutique firm and the support of a company that has more that $200 billion in assets under management and who's parent company (LFG) has been around for more than one hundred years.

I have written *The Power of a Plan* to help you understand the tremendous potential of comprehensive financial planning. Since 1992, I have incorporated this cross-disciplinary, collaborative approach into my professional practice. We like to refer to this approach as the Personal Chief Financial Officer or the "Personal CFO," You will find "the Personal CFO" concept and this comprehensive approach to planning described throughout the following chapters.

I hope this book helps you better understand the benefits of having an advisor who thinks like a "Personal CFO." In addition, I believe that each chapter will help you recognize the Power of a Plan in your own situation. Because of my professional affiliation with Lincoln and my association with the members of The Resource Group[1], I work with advisors throughout the country who believe and serve their clients like a Personal CFO. We often collaborate as we work with different individuals and business owners throughout the United States.

Since I will be referring to the practices of my own firm throughout the book, here's a little additional background about my firm. Stone Consulting Group was established in 2005 and is located in Roseville, California, a prosperous suburban city northeast of Sacramento. The atmosphere in my office is far from Wall Street. It's all warm colors, smiles, and personal greetings. We're in professional suites that overlook an upscale outdoor shopping mall; our clients really enjoy this fun and relaxing atmosphere. I'm an educator at heart, having spoken at numerous industry and corporate meetings. In addition, I served on the faculty of the University of California, Davis Extension, teaching other financial planners the benefits of doing planning on a comprehensive basis. In addition, I love to draw pictures that might help a client understand the concepts behind what's happening to their money. This book is written in the same spirit.

---

1   The Resource Group (TRG) is an invitation-only, nationwide network of the top two hundred planners within LFA. The goal of TRG is to collaborate, share intellectual capital—including financial-planning expertise, resources, networking opportunities, and practice-management strategies—and partner with Lincoln home office executives and committee concierge support to help drive practice development among advisors and provide industry-leading service to clients.

CHAPTER 1

THE PERSONAL CFO

WHAT YOU SHOULD EXPECT FROM A CERTIFIED FINANCIAL PLANNER™

In my family, sometimes my wife, Sabrina, and I joke around about our roles. I'm the main breadwinner, which makes me the chief financial officer, or CFO. And of course Sabrina is the boss, the CEO, and also the chief operating officer, or COO, because she truly runs our household, and she does it really well. I am not sure how it works in your home, but this is how it usually goes in the Stone home.

Of course, sometimes I think that I am the CEO too. When that happens, Sabrina likes to remind me of a line in the 2002 movie *My Big Fat Greek Wedding*. You know the line already, don't you? The main character, Toula, is upset because her father is making her feel guilty for having a desire to leave the family business. He keeps reminding her that he is the head of the family, and it is making her upset. Her mother hears their discussion and later says, "Let me tell you something, Toula, the man is the head [of the family], *but* the woman is the neck, and she can turn the head any way she wants." Of course, it never happens like that in the Stone family.

In a business, you, as the owner or senior partner, are sometimes the CEO, the CFO, and the COO and often more. We all have support from our employees, but in the end, it is the business owner's responsibility to make sure that everything is done right, that your customers are taken care of, and that they love you and the services or products you provide.

In a larger corporation, what is a CFO typically in charge of? A corporate CFO's job is to control the cash-flow position throughout the company, to understand the sources and uses of cash, and to maintain the integrity of those funds. Next most important, the CFO is responsible for company liabilities. The CFO may oversee department supervision and employee benefits, coordinating with the human resources department. The CFO may be in charge of financial relationships or financing or raising capital for the company and making sure that all financial obligations are paid. The CFO may be in charge of record control or shareholder relations or even budgeting or expense control.

Most smaller businesses and professional practices may hire a bookkeeper or an accountant but aren't large enough to justify hiring a dedicated corporate CFO. In the end, you, the owner, are responsible for your business. The same is true for your personal needs. The reality is that most successful people truly need a Personal CFO even if they do or don't have a corporate CFO.

THE FINANCIAL-PLANNING WHEEL OF FORTUNE

One of the most popular game shows ever on American television focuses on a roulette-style wheel of fortune and a puzzle. In real life, solving the puzzle of financial planning isn't a game and shouldn't involve gambling, but you can envision it through a different kind of wheel of fortune, with you in the center of the wheel.

THE FINANCIAL-PLANNING WHEEL OF FORTUNE

Around the outside of the wheel are all of your different advisors—CPA, attorney, investment advisor, insurance agent, real estate agent—as well as all of the other financial issues that you face as someone fortunate enough to enjoy success in your business or profession. These issues include tax, legal, investment, insurance, real estate, and generational wealth issues, along with other unique financial-planning areas depending on your situation. Since you are in the middle of the wheel, you are responsible for understanding all of the different issues that surround you, your family, and your business or professional practice. It's not any one person's job to oversee the entire financial situation. That's where the Personal CFO comes in.

As you look at the financial-planning wheel of fortune, the Personal CFO joins you in the center of that wheel, coordinating with all the other advisors to enable you to make and carry out your comprehensive financial plan. A Personal CFO essentially helps you connect the dots in your Financial-Planning Wheel of Fortune. In addition, this type of advisor helps you oversee all of your planning on a cross-disciplinary basis, not just from a tax, legal, insurance, or investment perspective but across the board. The advisor who incorporates the Personal CFO concept will help you create a strategy and carry out your financial and business plan by collaborating with your other expert advisors, such as your attorney and accountant. The Personal CFO is not there to take the place of your specialists, like your CPA or tax attorney, but to complement the work that they have done and to work in concert with them. It is very important that you trust your Personal CFO is a team player in addition to being someone with a high level of financial knowledge and personal integrity.

WHO NEEDS A PERSONAL CFO?

The type of individual who really needs a Personal CFO is a business owner or professional specialist who is successful—and very busy. Over twenty years of helping successful families and business owners, we have found that credentialed professionals such as doctors, dentists, attorneys, and CPAs especially appreciate the benefit of having someone in the center of that wheel to help assist them in getting their financial house in order. All types of business owners benefit from having a Personal CFO with whom to collaborate to make decisions that will help change their financial life and help them reach their financial goals, hopes, and dreams.

So how do you find an advisor who is like a Personal CFO? You may think that all financial advisors do this kind of coordinating and collaborating, but I have found over the years that it is *not* common. I began to realize this in the mid-1990s, as a result of an experience that began with me calling an estate-planning attorney for one of my clients. I wanted to find out specifically how the attorney wanted our client to hold title on a life insurance policy.

When the attorney answered the phone, I introduced myself and asked a question regarding our shared client's proposed life insurance policy and beneficiary designation. After I asked the question, there was complete silence on the other end of the phone, and his response to me was, "Who are you?" Confused, I thought maybe I had called the wrong attorney. After I was able to confirm that he was indeed the attorney for my client, I introduced myself again and then said, "I'm just calling to coordinate with you. I want to make sure that we get the beneficiary designations and the ownership set up properly for the life insurance on our client." The response I got was a surprise. The attorney didn't answer my question about the insurance but instead asked me, "Would you have lunch with me?" This was just a couple years after I graduated, and I felt a little uncomfortable, not knowing what to expect from this lunch with a successful attorney. We met at a restaurant convenient to both of our offices, got acquainted, discussed the client, and determined that our original plans to set up the insurance ownership and beneficiary designations were in line with the attorney's recommendations.

The attorney then said, "You're probably wondering why I wanted to have lunch with you." I responded, "Well, yes. I thought maybe you'd want to try to have me refer clients to you." He said, "That would be fine, but that's not why I wanted to talk to you. Tell me what you do." I explained what I have already told you, basically describing the concept of a Personal CFO and the Financial-Planning Wheel of Fortune. What he said next was, "Well, how are you paid?" I explained to him that I am paid as any other professional in the financial-services industry. His response was surprising. In fact, his response shaped the way that I built my business over the succeeding twenty-plus years.

He said, "For the past thirteen years I've been an estate-planning attorney, and during this time, you are the first financial planner, investment advisor, insurance agent, or real estate agent who has ever proactively contacted me to coordinate about any of my clients with regard to these sorts of issues." My response was, "You've got to be kidding me! I thought that everyone was doing planning like this." And he said, "Unfortunately, no. That's been my experience." Then he said, "What about me?" And I said, "I'm not sure I understand. What do you mean, 'What about you?'" And he responded, "Will you be *my* advisor?"

Here was a business owner who owns a law firm, who's a successful, busy person. He's a specialist in legal matters, specifically in estate and business owner planning, and he saw the value of collaborating with a Personal CFO on all aspects of his financial life. He also liked the idea about coordinating with his CPA while assisting him in organizing and coordinating his personal and business owner planning.

Since the time he became a client, I've had many opportunities to meet with other professionals who were advising my clients, such as their CPAs and attorneys. When given the opportunity, I would ask them about their experiences with other financial advisors and introduce them to the Personal CFO concept. What I heard from each professional reinforced my belief in the value of an advisor focused on coordinating and planning, instead of someone who's just trying to sell financial products.

THE MONEY MAKEOVER

For six years, I served on the board of directors of the Financial Planning Association of Northern California. During this time, I had many opportunities to be involved in different initiatives and service opportunities. One of those service opportunities happened in the fall of 2000 and involved the *Sacramento Bee*, the daily newspaper in California's capital city. The board agreed to do pro bono financial planning for some of the newspaper's readers for a series of monthly "Money Makeovers" stories. Readers would write a letter about why they wanted free financial planning. As a volunteer, I received a batch of letters, interviewed a few of the applicants, and chose a suburban couple, Ronald and Brookelea Lutton.

After an initial consultation, we concluded that it was a good fit. The next meeting was our Discovery meeting, the primary data-gathering meeting for a client who is creating a financial plan. The *Bee* reporter joined us, and we went through our normal process. Within a few weeks, I was delivering a completed financial plan in a meeting in which the reporter frantically took notes. At the end of our meeting, I asked him, "Do you have any more questions?" He responded, "No. I don't have any more questions at this point. You've answered all my questions so far, but I would like to make a comment." At this point, I was concerned. What had I gotten myself into? What had I done? He turned to Mr. and Mrs. Lutton, and he said, "I want you to know that my experience has shown me that individuals who have an advisor that does comprehensive financial planning are most likely to uncover opportunities to improve their financial standing."

Of course, I was thrilled to hear that, and it gave me one more reason to feel confident that the Personal CFO approach truly is benefiting the clients. I am a big believer in teamwork. I believe that the triangle of advisors—the CPA, the attorney, and the advisor acting as the Personal CFO—will truly help the client make better decisions. By you providing your team all of the necessary data and having them put their collective minds together, those united advisors can help the clients have a better chance of reaching their long-term or short-term goals and objectives.

TOUGH SURPRISES

Unfortunately, I've had people ask me for help with problems resulting from a lack of communication between their advisors and, in some cases, even between advisor and client. One woman was referred to me by one of my clients after she found out she had to pay over $70,000 in capital gains taxes, a surprise result of her stockbroker reallocating her investments. My first question was, "Well, what did your CPA say? Did your investment advisor coordinate and collaborate with your CPA?" And the woman informed me that, no, her accountant figured out the tax liability after she showed him the 1099, her copy of a form reporting her investment income to the IRS.

When you have your planning done on a cross-disciplinary basis with the Personal CFO approach, it not only opens up lines of communication between the members of your advisory team but also provides an impetus to action for the client. It isn't just sitting back and saying, "What do we do next?" In comprehensive planning, the key is what you do to implement that plan. If you are a business owner and never followed through with the Personal CFO's recommendations, then it is very difficult for you to see their value.

It is important that you have a strong team. We have had some really great experiences with our clients' CPAs and attorneys over the years. We love working with them. Many, seeing the value of a coordinated team and the benefit of the Financial-Planning Wheel of Fortune, have even become clients. There are many reasons why your Personal CFO should enjoy this professional team approach—it introduces your Personal CFO to other prospective clients, and it provides organized professional collaboration, to name two. I personally appreciate the latter benefit the most because it helps your team know that they are helping you make the right decisions, much like we did with the attorney back in the mid-1990s.

The CPAs or attorneys who work most successfully in this team approach are organized, easy to reach, and not territorial about their areas of expertise. By and large, my experience has been positive in working with other professionals and collaborating with them. Because of my background in college and high school sports, I have the opinion that a team player is a great player, and hopefully your advisors are team players. If you are concerned that they're not, then your Personal CFO should be able to refer you to other professionals who are.

THE MOST FREQUENTLY ASKED QUESTION

Q. Why do I need a "Personal CFO" if I already have competent advisors handling my accounting, investments, and legal affairs?

A. The answer is simply coordination, or more specifically, avoiding a lack of coordination that may be limiting the potential benefits of the planning you already are doing. A Personal CFO helping you experience the Power of a Plan will look at your entire financial picture at once. They will look at your financial situation on a cross-disciplinary basis—not just from a legal or accounting perspective but across the board. This allows them to identify both coordination gaps and opportunities to take the planning to a higher level. My experience has been that those individuals who work with an advisor who does planning like a Personal CFO have had more successful results. We believe that the difference between merely having their work done versus having it done as well as possible provides confidence in their planning and the opportunity for a retention of more money for themselves and their heirs depending on the situation.

WHAT TO EXPECT FROM A FINANCIAL PLANNER

Some of my friends and clients have asked me why I am sharing our planning process in this book. Well, the bottom line is that this process works. Many financial planners do not go through all the necessary steps to do comprehensive financial planning like the Personal CFO. Many also do not collaborate with other professional advisors, and that can potentially be a detriment to the client's overall results. In fact, my experience has been that by having your Personal CFO work in a collaborative effort with your accountant and attorney, it can make a significant impact on your ability to both identify and reach your long-term financial and business owner planning goals. My experience has been that those individuals who work with an advisor who does planning like a Personal CFO have had more successful results. In fact, most have found that the difference between merely having their work done versus having it done as well as possible can mean greater confidence in their planning and a significant amount of money to themselves and their heirs depending on the situation.

The relationship between you and your Personal CFO should start with you getting to know each other. This communication allows your advisor ultimately to assist you in identifying both coordination gaps as well as planning opportunities. The Power of a Plan cannot be truly realized if your Personal CFO is not a good listener. Without two-way communication, neither of you will be able to understand your long- and short-term goals.

I would like to take you through an example of the initial planning process to give you an idea of what you ought to be looking for in your interviews as you consider working with different financial advisors. This is the Personal CFO process we use at Stone Consulting Group, but the education can be used as a reference wherever you conduct your search for a Personal CFO who will work with or help you create your advisory team.

In your initial consultation, which I call the "concept interview," the planner should be learning about your situation, with more talk about you than them. But you will want to find out what they do and how it helps you, asking such questions as:

- Do they do the sort of things that a Personal CFO would do?

- Are they involved in budgeting?

- Are they involved in helping you with your risk management and your insurance?

- Are they involved in helping you with your investment management?

- Do they help you not only with retirement planning but also with retirement distribution planning? (We'll get into that distinction later in the book.)

- Do they know and understand how to deal with real estate issues?

- Do they have the ability to help you with generational wealth issues?

- Can they help you by coordinating and collaborating with your other advisors when it comes to tax planning and estate planning?

During your initial consultation, the advisor should help you understand how they are paid and how that might affect you. Compensation can come either through fees or commissions, depending on the products or services that are involved for your plan implementation. Most financial planning is done on a fee basis. If they don't charge a fee, then they need to make a living somehow, so they'll try to sell you a product on commission.

THE FINANCIAL-PLANNING PROCESS

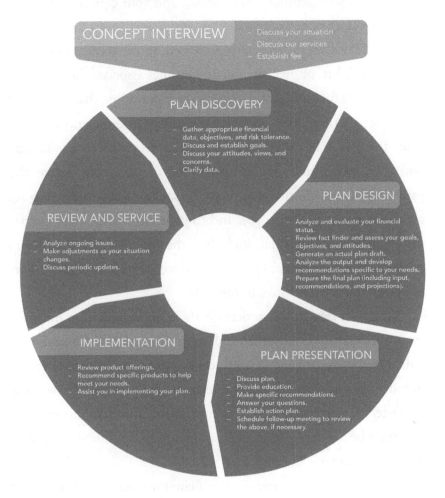

Once you have decided to hire your new advisor, the next planning step is Discovery. This is key to the your professional experience. We call it Discovery because you will be asked questions that you probably haven't been asked before, and together you and your advisor will discover the answers to these questions. One of the primary reasons for this meeting is to help you crystalize your financial vision for now and into the future. In addition, the Discovery meeting is where your Personal CFO and team gather all of your appropriate financial data, discuss your goals and objectives and your risk tolerance, and then discuss your attitudes, your views, and your concerns, and help clarify any data that you provided in your initial consultation.

The Plan Design step takes place behind the scenes, where your advisor and his or her financial-planning associates analyze and evaluate your financial status, review the fact finding that they did in the prior meetings, and assess your goals, objectives, and attitudes. Then the first draft of your plan is created. In most cases, your team will go through at least a couple drafts of your plan before they present it to you. In the plan, your Personal CFO will develop recommendations specific to you and to your family. They will prepare the financial plan, in final, including the input, recommendations, projections, and forecasts for where you would be in the future if you continue to do what you're doing now.

The next step in this process is the Plan Presentation, in which your Personal CFO goes through your plan and discusses it with you. He should provide you education along with specific recommendations and answers to any questions that you might have. With advancements in technology, it is now possible to have this plan presentation be a dynamic experience showing many different variables, depending on your questions.

Ultimately, at the end of the Plan Presentation, your advisor should create an action plan with an implementation schedule based on their recommendations. In addition, you will have the option to choose how you want your Personal CFO and his team to help you do those things listed on the implementation schedule. The plan will also identify who's responsible for getting the tasks done and what the target date is for each item. Ultimately, the Personal CFO and his team will track when that work is done so that you will know your progress. After moving through the implementation process, they should review and recommend specific product offerings to help you meet your needs and assist you in implementing your plan.

At this point, you are probably wondering how your Personal CFO gets paid. The Personal CFO is usually compensated in three ways. The first is the fee for the planning and data-gathering services just described. At most companies, the fee includes the initial plan and a year's worth of service on that plan from your Personal CFO. At the end of the year, most advisors sit down with their clients, make any necessary updates, and determine what ongoing work, if any, needs to be done. Typically, renewal fees should run anywhere from 50 percent to 100 percent of your Personal CFO's current fee schedule.

The second way that your Personal CFO is paid has to do with the implementation of your plan. Most advisors should show you several strategies to improve your situation and help you reach your goals. Some of these strategies may include the use of financial products such as insurance or professionally managed investments. The Personal CFO will usually represent his or her clients in the financial-product marketplaces. Acting as your advocate, a Personal CFO should do that work as professionally as everything else, making sure that what he or she brings you is competitive and, most importantly, ensuring that it fits your plan. Your Personal CFO would earn a commission or a fee for that service, just like anyone else.

The third component of a Personal CFO's fee structure is not a fee at all but rather an act of goodwill on your part. There's no money that changes hands here, but many consider this the most meaningful source of compensation. Once you can say, "I can't believe what an exceptional job you've done," to your Personal CFO, then they typically will ask for your help in identifying and introducing them to other people who may also benefit from their work.

The following chapters address personal and business-planning concepts or questions that each of you should ask yourself with regard to your personal situation. I share with you some stories about client successes and disappointments over the years. Hopefully these real-life experiences of some of our clients will motivate you to get your financial house in order and be more prepared.

CHAPTER 2

THE BASICS OF CASH MANAGEMENT

One of the main responsibilities of a corporate CFO is to oversee and to help control cash flow. The same is true when you have a financial advisor acting as your Personal CFO. It is just as important for you to understand your personal expenditures as it is for you as a business owner to know you have financial resources. Over the years, I have sometimes had clients resist taking a really close look at their own spending. Some call it "budgeting," but the idea of being on a budget has a somewhat negative connotation. I like to call it a "spending plan" because clients like to spend money.

When you earn a dollar, either by working or having your assets earn that dollar, the IRS and most state governments want a piece of that dollar. We come back to taxes in more detail in chapter 7. What's left after taxes is your net investable income, money you can either save or spend. If you take the time to know what is being spent and what is being saved, you can do a better job of maximizing your ability to grow your assets for you and your family.

Some of my clients feel too busy to make a spending plan, or they have a substantial income and aren't worried about knowing where the excess is going. They say, "We spend what we want to spend." So I let them know that, in that case, they can increase the money they are putting away as savings. As we keep doing that, eventually they say they feel like they are running out of spending money and can't save any more. I ask, "How do you know?" And that brings us back to their need for a spending plan.

A working spending plan helps us measure reality—to increase our likelihood of having reasonable and appropriate goals, whether it is forecasting cash flow for a business or our personal lives. A few years ago, while sitting down with my wife, Sabrina, to update our own financial plan, we were both really surprised to see how inflation and changes in the Stone family—for example, three children in college—had impacted our spending plan.

The importance of a strong understanding of your cash management becomes more apparent when you begin to address the many different aspects of a comprehensive financial plan. Let's focus on the factors that go into personal cash flow, although the same approach is just as critical for a business.

UNDERSTANDING YOUR CASH FLOW

To understand your cash flow, it's helpful to divide income and expenses into these categories (See a sample budget in Appendix D.):

INCOME SOURCES

- **Fixed Income.** Includes reliable income from salary, Social Security, employer pensions, private pensions, rental property, or other sources.

- **Variable Income.** Might include bonus compensation, or if you're the owner of a business, company profit or quarterly distributions or draws.

EXPENSES

- **Fixed monthly expenses.** Includes mortgages and car payments. For a business owner, it could be the rent that you're paying for your office space.

- **Variable monthly expenses.** Includes utilities, groceries, gasoline—things you need on a monthly basis but for which spending goes up and down through the year.

- **Fixed nonmonthly expenses.** Could include life and auto insurance premiums and personal or business property taxes.

- **Variable nonmonthly expenses.** Includes your home maintenance, charitable contributions, gifts, and other spending that is not monthly and may come up once a year. I know Christmas is big for some families. It is for mine.

- **Invisible expenses.** When your water heater breaks down, or when you need major car repairs or new tires or brakes, or when your roof needs to be fixed or replaced, these are invisible expenses if you have not anticipated them in your plan. These invisible expenses can sometimes drive us into debt.

- **Planned savings.** This is when you're putting money away monthly or yearly for college, weddings, or retirement, or just building your cash reserves.

Most financial professionals recommend that you keep an emergency cash reserve that represents approximately three to six months of your expenses. There are many good reasons to do this, but the most important is to avoid going into debt to cover those financial surprises. Where do you save or invest these reserve funds? The answer is really a personal one for each individual client, but in every case these funds should be fully liquid, with limited risk to the principal and no cost to you to move money into or out of the account.

Sometimes clients will have excess income and a desire to put it to work. They will often ask me about ideas to improve their rate of return on investments. A client once had excess cash of $20,000 set aside in an emergency reserve. She asked me where I thought she should invest her funds. I discussed an amazing investment opportunity that comes up from time to time when working with clients like her. I will sometimes refer to this opportunity as one of the greatest investments of all time. I told the client the rate of return was 21 percent guaranteed and it was tax-free. Isn't that great? How many of you would be interested in that investment? I recommended that this client take all $20,000 and put $9,000 into an investment called VISA and the remaining $11,000 into an investment called Master-Card. Yes, you're right. We saved 21 percent guaranteed tax-free by

paying off credit cards where she had a balance. She actually came into the office and cut up her credit cards, and I still have them in a bag in my office today.

As an unknown wise individual once said: "Those who understand interest earn it. Those who don't understand interest pay it."

TWO TYPES OF DEBT

There are two different types of debt—revolving debt and amortized debt. Revolving debt would include things like a balance on your credit cards or an automobile loan. The amount of interest that you pay on that loan goes down as you reduce the amount of debt that you have. An amortized debt would be something like your mortgage. In a loan where there is an amortization schedule, the amount of interest that you will pay each month is already established by contract. Many people think if they put extra principal down against their mortgage that they'll pay less interest. Well, that is true if you carry the mortgage to the end of its full term. If you have a thirty-year mortgage and pay it off completely in twenty-seven years because you have prepaid some principal, then you will save some money on interest—in fact, you will save a lot!

If you don't carry the mortgage to full term—meaning you either sell your home before you pay off the mortgage or you refinance the mortgage—you save exactly zero dollars in interest on the money you put down to reduce your loan. When you get a loan to buy a property, an amortization schedule is determined from day one of that mortgage. In other words, your contract with the lender-specific states exactly what the interest payment will be each month of the mortgage. The same is true as it relates to the specific dollar amount that is dedicated to principal each month. If your loan is an interest only loan, the dynamics of your choices change. There are pros and cons to paying down your mortgage early. As you work with your advisor, paying down your revolving credit usually comes first. It typically has a higher interest rate, and the rate is based on the remaining balance as you pay it down. The tax deductibility of your interest should also be taken into account while you analyze your options. Your Personal CFO should assist you in making customized decisions as it relates to debt elimination.

Current interest rates are low from a historical perspective, so now might be as good a time as any to do a fixed-rate mortgage versus an adjustable-rate mortgage. But your Personal CFO should take into account your situation. If you know you are going to be moving in five years, an adjustable-rate mortgage that is fixed for an initial period of five years will usually give you a lower rate. However, I would ask you if you had considered the risks involved: "What if something changes in your plans?" Suppose your plan was to move to Arizona, but you chose to stay in California in the same home. Now you have an adjustable-rate mortgage, and five years from now, who knows where interest rates will be.

TERMS OF MORTGAGES

Thirty years is the most common term for paying off home mortgages in the United States. The longer the term, the higher the interest rate, typically. The shorter the term, the lower the interest rate. It's important to know what you can really, truly afford. A mortgage specialist or your Personal CFO can help you understand this. Many times, the banks will qualify you for more than you should really be spending on a mortgage, especially if you have other priorities such as putting money away for emergencies or building your business. If you have completed your spending plan, as discussed earlier, this will also help you make the right cash-management decisions.

EXAMPLES OF A BETTER WAY TO SAVE ON YOUR MORTGAGE INTEREST

If you borrowed $500,000 on a thirty-year mortgage at 4 percent interest, your mortgage payment, principal, and interest would be $2,387.08 per month. If you paid that mortgage for the full thirty years, you would have paid $859,347.53, including interest. If you borrowed money using a fifteen-year mortgage at the same 4 percent rate, your monthly payment would increase to $3,698.44 per month, but the total you would pay over fifteen years would be only $665,719.13. That is a big savings (almost 23 percent) if you can come up with a little over $1,300 more each month. In addition, the interest rate is likely to be lower on a fifteen-year mortgage, so the benefits would be even greater than previously stated.

Alternatively, if you really want to get your mortgage paid off sooner, you could choose a ten-year loan. If you choose a ten-year loan, the interest rate would likely be lower than the fifteen- or thirty-year mortgages. If the rate were 3.5 percent, your monthly payment would be $4,944.29. Your total cost to pay off the same $500,000 loan would be only $593,315.20, so the amount of interest on the mortgage is $93,315 compared with $359,347.53 for the thirty-year mortgage. Do you remember the previous quote? "Those who understand interest earn it. Those who don't understand interest pay it." Do you understand interest?

LINES OF CREDIT

Lines of credit can be secured by collateral such as your home equity, or unsecured. Depending on the uses of that credit, the interest you pay can be either deductible or nondeductible from your income taxes. For a personal line of credit, don't assume the interest is deductible just because you are spending money on your home or real estate. If it's a business line of credit and you're using it to build your small business, then it is likely that the interest will be deductible. But you or your Personal CFO should be checking with your CPA on the current tax law.

INTEREST ARBITRAGE

If you borrow money from a line of credit at 3 percent interest and put it into an investment for which the interest is nondeductible, you might be able to earn more than that 3 percent. If your investment pays 5 percent and you keep the 2 percent difference, that's the arbitrage. Be careful with an arbitrage strategy because if three or four years later your investment starts paying less, your arbitrage can suddenly turn negative. This is a dangerous strategy and is often not worth taking the risk to borrow money to invest.

THE BUYING-UP PROBLEM

Let's say someone was making $100,000 a year; they get a raise, and now they're making $106,000 a year. The person thinks, *Now I can go out and buy something with a payment that is $500 a month.* So they lease a new car. What they should do with those excess funds is (1) pay down debt, (2) build up reserves, and then (3) begin to save and invest in some areas we will cover in the coming chapters. I'm a big believer in "paying yourself first." But save for something you can use later, not a depreciating asset like a car or a TV that goes down in value the day you bring it home.

It's important that you understand the different aspects of cash management for your small-business or family finances. Knowing what you're spending, how you're spending it, what you're saving, and what you can afford to save enables you to accomplish your financial hopes and dreams. Remember the client who cut up her credit cards in my office? She'd previously met with a bankruptcy attorney to deal with debt that came from overspending inheritance. By meeting with me and making a spending plan that matched the monthly income and distributions she was receiving from investments, we helped her stick to her spending plan. Now she is out of credit card debt and feels a huge weight has been lifted off her financial shoulders.

In the next chapter, we discuss something most people can't afford not to buy.

CHAPTER 3

MANAGING RISK AND INSURANCE STRATEGIES

I was updating a client's financial plan a few years ago and made a worrisome discovery. The client, Steve, needed another million dollars of death benefit to prevent his wife, Sharon, from having to return to work if something were to happen to him. We researched different companies to provide the coverage for him and his family. Steve had stopped smoking a couple months before, but none of the companies would offer the substantially lower nonsmoker rate until he was a nonsmoker for at least twelve months. I recommended that he buy the life insurance as a smoker and reduce his premiums to nonsmoker rates later when he could pass a urinalysis exam to prove that there was no nicotine in his system.

Steve decided to wait ten more months and then apply for nonsmoker rates. I told him, "You never know what is going to happen to your health. We may not be able to get the same coverage ten months from now." He said that he understood, and we agreed to follow up during the next yearly update of his financial plan. A few months later, I got a call from Steve. He informed me that he had recently been diagnosed with cancer. Of course, I was saddened by the news. As I stood, looking out my office window, Steve informed me that the first thing that came to his mind when he received the diagnosis were my words, ringing in his ears: "Steve, you never know what is going to happen with your health." This was a life-changing moment for me as an advisor, reinforcing the need to focus on the foundation of the planning pyramid, which I explain in this chapter. I questioned myself over and over again about what I could have done differently. Could I have helped him understand? Sadly, Steve passed away a few weeks later, and Sharon was left with two young boys and had to go back to work.

FINANCIAL-PLANNING PYRAMID

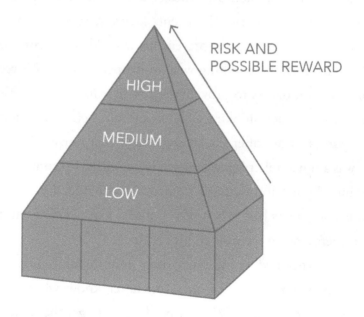

THE FINANCIAL-PLANNING PYRAMID

Over the years, I have used pictures to help clients better understand financial concepts. One of those pictures I call the financial-planning pyramid. Three horizontal lines divide the pyramid, creating sections for low-, medium-, and high-risk investments. The higher we go up the pyramid, the higher the risk and the higher the opportunity for reward. The section at the foundation of the pyramid is devoted to risk management—managing the personal risks that significantly affect all of us. Before we can talk about investing for wealth gain, we have to cover these personal risks and discuss different types of insurance.

FINANCIAL-PLANNING PYRAMID

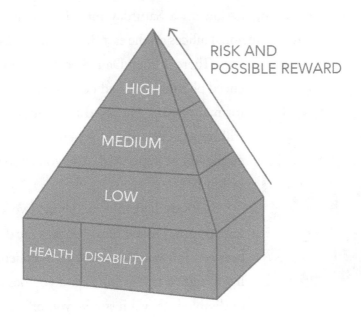

SICKNESS AND INJURY

As a father of five, I've made many visits to doctors and hospitals. In 1988, my wife and I had our first child, and because we had good health insurance, we owed the hospital only a $5 co-pay. When my youngest child was born in 2001, unfortunately my wife and my son spent seven weeks in the hospital between them, and the bill was in the hundreds of thousands of dollars. Without health insurance, we would have been financially devastated; that is why a good health insurance policy is a very important part of the financial-planning pyramid's foundation. Health insurance protects against a catastrophic loss. We talk more about it in chapter 10, which addresses how a business owner deals with employee benefits.

DISABILITY

In 1992, starting work full time as a professional financial advisor, I attended a training session on a Saturday morning at the Lincoln Financial Advisors regional offices on the east side of the San Francisco

Dan Steckbeck

Bay. There I met Dan Steckbeck, an experienced planner who had been with the company for many years. He asked me a question that I still remember today: "When you signed your employment paperwork, did you choose Job A or Job B?"

Nobody had told me about two different job options. I asked him, "What's the difference between Job A and Job B?" Dan replied, "Well, if you signed up for Job A and you become sick or disabled, they'll just take you off the payroll. Then you won't have a job anymore." I said, "Okay, well, I think that's the one I chose." Then I said, "So what is Job B?" Dan said, "Well, if you chose Job B, they will end up paying you a few thousand dollars a year less for exactly the same work that you're doing in Job A. But if for some reason you become sick or disabled and can't continue to work, they'll keep you on the company payroll, and you'll receive an income until you're age sixty-five." I responded, "Dan, you've got to be kidding me. That sounds too good to be true. What's the catch?" He said, "There is no catch." So I asked him, "How can I get Job B?" He replied, "You can buy disability insurance on yourself."

It became clear to me that all he was talking about was taking the time and effort to research and purchase a disability policy to protect my income for my family. Disability insurance replaces income when a sickness or injury is long term and we lose our ability to work. In the end, I did choose Job B. Fortunately, I have not had to use the disability insurance I have owned since 1992. I have had experience with clients who have chosen "Job B," and it provided protection at a time they needed it.

Many years ago, I had the "Job A/Job B" discussion with one client, William, just like Dan and I did in 1992. Since William was a chiropractor, he truly understood the concept because he saw so many patients who had become disabled. It greatly changed their lives financially. Because of his experience, William chose a "Cadillac version" disability policy. I remember asking him whether he could really afford to purchase such a high-end policy. His response was, "Maybe I can't afford to have this kind of a policy, but David, I really can't afford *not* to purchase a disability policy of this quality."

About five years later, his wife informed me that William was in a serious car accident while driving in the fog. With this "Cadillac" disability policy, the insurance company was able to provide him an income for a couple of years while he recovered from his injuries, including a partial disability benefit that helped William transition back into his practice. Shortly after he went back to work, he thanked me for looking out for him and his family, saying: "This disability plan saved my business. It saved my home and probably saved my marriage, too."

FINANCIAL-PLANNING PYRAMID

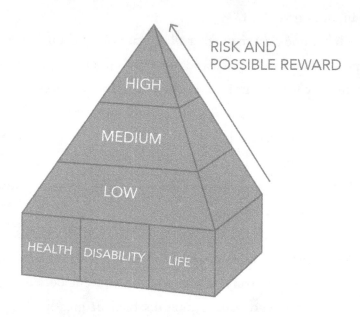

RISK AND
POSSIBLE REWARD

HIGH

MEDIUM

LOW

HEALTH   DISABILITY   LIFE

LIFE INSURANCE . . . RENTING VS. OWNING

The third area of risk management at the foundation of your financial-planning pyramid is your survivorship planning and life insurance. Even though the statistical likelihood of becoming disabled before age sixty-five is higher than the likelihood of dying before age sixty-five, more people buy life insurance than disability insurance. I believe that this is primarily due to the fact that there are more insurance companies and agents who sell life insurance than sell disability insurance policies. As you review the survivorship needs of your family or business associates, working with a Personal CFO who understands your complete plan will provide a better chance of making the right choice for you and your family. There are many questions for your Personal CFO to address with you relating to your current needs for life insurance.

Some questions to think about:

- What kind of financial life do you want your family to experience if your life ends abruptly?

- What type of standard of living do you want to provide?

- Will they have to sell the family residence, or will they be able to pay off the mortgage?

- What about your lines of credit?

- Will they need or want to sell the family business? And what is it worth?

- Are enough funds set aside for your children's weddings or college education?

- Do you want your spouse to have to go back to work?

- How much life insurance do you need?

TWO PRIMARY TYPES OF LIFE INSURANCE

Another question to consider is how long you need life insurance, which is something you can either own or rent, like real estate. When you rent your insurance, it's much like you're renting your home or your office. You have a period of time, as in a lease, during which you keep that life insurance, which is known as term insurance. It's usually the less expensive alternative for those who have a short-term need. You can buy term insurance for a ten-, fifteen-, twenty-, or thirty-year period, depending on your age.

As in real estate, there are pros and cons to owning versus renting life insurance. Owning your home is usually more expensive than renting because you, rather than a landlord, pay the ongoing costs such as upkeep and property taxes. When you own your life insurance, it usually does cost you more because just like paying down a mortgage on a home in hopes of building equity, you are putting money in a life insurance policy in hopes of building cash value.

You can at any time, if you choose, take cash out of that policy, just like you can borrow money against your home equity. Once you've paid off your home mortgage, you can live in that home for the rest of your life and then give it to your kids. In the case of a life insurance policy that you own, you can keep it for the rest of your life and pass it on to your spouse or heirs. There are tax benefits for owning life insurance, much like there are tax benefits for owning your residence.

The type of life insurance that you own, "permanent insurance," comes in different products and programs, including whole life, universal life, variable universal life, and indexed universal life. You can own some of your life insurance and rent some, too. The equivalent in real estate, though not very common, is owning your home and renting the one next door. How much life insurance you would own and how much you would rent is very personalized. Your Personal CFO can help you find the best solution, which in many cases is a customized combination of term and permanent. It is not "one size fits all," despite what some commentators say on radio or TV.

FINANCIAL-PLANNING PYRAMID

RISK AND
POSSIBLE REWARD

HIGH

MEDIUM

LOW

HEALTH   DISABILITY   LIFE   LTC

LONG-TERM CARE

The fourth area of risk management at the foundation of the financial-planning pyramid is the risk of needing long-term care. The risk in retirement of long-term health care creating a significant financial burden on you and your family is well documented. According to the US Department of Health and Human Services, someone turning sixty-five today has almost a 70 percent chance of needing some type of long-term care services and support in their remaining years.[2] This is different from being disabled for purposes of work and affects anyone who needs care in home or care at a nursing home for the activities of daily living (ADLs). The ADLs, as defined by the US

2 "How Much Care Will You Need?", U.S. Department of
Health and Human Services, http://longtermcare.gov/the-basics/
how-much-care-will-you-need/.

government, are: bathing, dressing, using the toilet, transferring (to or from bed or chair), eating, and caring for incontinence.[3]

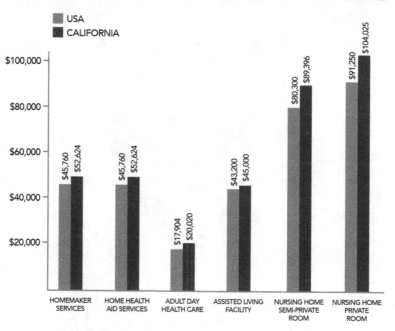

MEDIAN ANNUAL COSTS FOR LONG-TERM CARE

According to the same US Department of Health and Human Services, the average time that women need long-term care services is 3.7 years, compared to 2.2 years for men.[4] Either way, the costs associated with care for those who struggle with the activities of daily living are very expensive. Genworth Financial, Inc. does a survey annually on the different costs for care throughout the United States. The survey breaks down the expenses from adult day-care services all the way to the costs of a private room in a nursing home. I can't really

3   "What Is Long-Term Care?", U.S. Department of Health and Human Services, http://longtermcare.gov/the-basics/what-is-long-term-care/.

4   "How Much Care Will You Need?", U.S. Department of Health and Human Services, http://longtermcare.gov/the-basics/how-much-care-will-you-need/.

do the survey justice in this chapter since it is so comprehensive. However, suffice it to say the average cost in the United States ranges from $17,904 per year for the cost of adult day care (five days per week) to $91,250 per year for a private room in a nursing home. The median costs in California are much higher.[5]

Now that we have established the possible financial risks associated with the need for long-term health care, I wanted to provide you a little more education on a few strategies that will help you create a plan for this potential financial liability. There are three basic ways to handle a need for long-term care. If you have a large net worth, you might be able to self-insure by setting aside money in specific accounts for this purpose. Second, you can purchase a standalone, long-term care insurance policy. You would pay premiums for the rest of your life. If you don't need the care, perhaps because you pass away in your sleep, then those dollars are gone. This option is much like "renting" your long-term care insurance. The third option, called a linked-benefit plan, is like a combination of option 1 and option 2.

Recently I was speaking with a new client who was paying about $3,500 per year for a long-term care policy he purchased a few years ago. If he lives thirty more years, surviving past age ninety with no need for long-term care, he would pay an additional $105,000 in premiums with the possibility that he and his heirs will receive nothing in return. He asked me if I thought it was a good idea for him to continue to pay these long-term care policy premiums.

In the early 2000s, insurance companies came up with the linked-benefit strategy. In the linked benefit, you are putting aside your own assets in an account and then providing those assets to an insurance company that covers you for long-term care. The insurance

---

5   "Genworth 2015 Cost of Care Survey California," Genworth, https://www.genworth.com/dam/Americas/US/PDFs/Consumer/corporate/cost-of-care/118928CA_040115_gnw.pdf.

companies are using a life insurance policy to provide a place for your funds. You have flexibility to determine how much benefit you want and how soon you want to start putting money away for that benefit. As always in financial planning, the earlier you start, the better—and the less money you need to set aside to reach your objective. In the end, if you never use the long-term care benefit, your heirs will receive the money that you set aside and a little more as a death benefit.

Another advantage of a linked-benefit strategy is that there is no waiting period to use your benefits. In a basic long-term care insurance policy, there is what's called an elimination period, commonly anywhere from 90 days to 365 days, before you have access to the benefits.

Your Personal CFO can help you determine which of these solutions makes sense. Depending on your individual situation, using a linked-benefit strategy can often be more cost effective than purchasing just a standalone, long-term care policy.

I have a client, age forty-nine, who is putting $90,000 into a linked benefit over five years, providing her $300,000 in long-term care benefits by the end of the five years. If she does not need long-term care until she is eighty-five, by then her insurance company would provide nearly $900,000 of long-term care. And if she died without using the long-term care, her heirs would get the $90,000 that she put in, plus a $50,000 death benefit. The $90,000 is her full premium in this insurance, and at any time after the five years, she can choose to receive a full return of her premium, or the value of the account, whichever is higher.

In the last few years, insurance companies have also introduced another type of linked benefit product that uses an annuity contract instead of a life insurance policy as the program's structure. The benefits are different than the programs that use a life insurance policy and will also vary by company as well as by type. It is important for you and your Personal CFO to do your research on the programs that are available. Linked-benefit policies are offered by only a few insurance companies, so not all advisors will know to suggest the strategy as an alternative to consider. The reality is, most financial advisors aren't licensed to sell long-term care insurance, and many do not get the additional education needed to be aware of such new products.

A CAUTIONARY TALE

Because insurance is such an important part of financial planning, it is important to recognize that the foundation of any financial strategy is understanding the risks we all take on a daily basis that could hurt us. With the permission of my brother-in-law, I will share a personal story. About five years ago, I received a call at 3:00 a.m. It was a social worker at UC Davis Medical Center in Sacramento, California, informing me that my sister, Kathy, and her husband, Kent, were in a serious car accident around midnight. My heart dropped as I was told that my sister was killed, and my brother-in-law was in critical condition in the intensive care unit. I went to the hospital to be with my sister's two youngest children, Jason and Christina.

When I went to my office later that Saturday afternoon, I looked up my sister's financial-planning file to see what, if any, life insurance they still had. I had recalled that eighteen months prior, Kent and Kathy had asked me and my staff about the necessity of keeping insurance on Kathy's life. I told them that I believed they should keep it, but that I understood they were trying to save money by eliminating the life insurance on Kathy. When I looked at the file, my memory was correct and my fears were confirmed. Though Kent and Kathy had decided to keep Kent's life insurance in force, their final decision was to cancel the insurance on Kathy's life. There would be no death claim paid to Kent and the children. The amount of the life insurance was substantial and would have provided a significant financial benefit to the family during the challenging time of Kent's recovery.

A few weeks later, when Kent was finally able to speak about the incident, one of the first things he said to me when we were alone in his hospital room was, "I guess it was a mistake for us to not keep that life insurance on Kathy." This statement was heart wrenching for me as I tried to formulate what I could have said eighteen months prior to have convinced them to keep the policy. Unfortunately, Kent's injuries made him unable to work, and ultimately, they lost their home. If they had the life insurance in force, Kent could have paid off the mortgage.

Kent's health has improved since the accident, and he is doing much better. However, the financial strain placed on him while he was healing from the accident made day-to-day life much more difficult than it would have been if the life insurance had remained in place. Fortunately, Kent did have health insurance to pay for the weeks in the ICU and the months of rehabilitation. He also had a disability policy that helped him maintain a standard of living by delivering monthly cash flow for the basic necessities of life. His disability policy continues to provide a benefit for him to this day.

This experience changed me forever. I was most impressed by the support and love shown by the members of their church and how they rallied around the family through acts of compassionate service. It was a blessing to see a community come together for the benefit of one of their friends. In the end, I am committed to helping my clients protect their financial lives with insurance planning and risk management.

In Risk Management, like all of the areas of comprehensive financial planning, it is important to prepare now as you plan to navigate the challenges and the opportunities of your financial lives. Life is not always smooth sailing, as we discuss in the next chapter on investing.

CHAPTER 4

ARE YOU SAILING OR ROWING OR BOTH?

A few years ago, my client Bruce and his wife Linda invited my family to go sailing. We met them on the east side of the San Francisco Bay and boarded his sailboat. It was a beautiful day, and there was only a slight breeze at the time. I wondered, *How are we going to sail without a strong wind?* Bruce started up an engine on the back of his sailboat and got us out into the bay, where the wind was really blowing. Our plan was to sail west toward the Pacific Ocean, under the Golden Gate Bridge, and then circle back into the bay. Since the wind was blowing right at us, I thought that our planned route was an impossible task.

How are we going to get to the Golden Gate Bridge if the wind's blowing in our faces? I wondered. I learned one of the first rules of

sailing: all you need is wind. It really doesn't even matter which direction the wind is blowing. However, if the wind isn't blowing, that's when you're in trouble.

In sailing vernacular, we began to tack back and forth, using the wind to push us left and right, driving us in a zigzag across the bay in the direction that we wanted to go.

We had a wonderful experience sailing past Alcatraz and through the Golden Gate, and it got me to thinking about how it reflects on the way people invest their money. Now, you may ask, "What do investing and sailing have in common?" Well, just like sailing, in investing the wind doesn't necessarily have to be at your back for you to be successful in reaching your final destination. However, if the wind is not blowing, then all you can do is drift with the current. The ups and downs of the stock market are like the blowing and waning wind for your portfolio. A company by the name of Crestmont Research originated the idea of comparing alternative investment solutions to sailing and rowing.[6] I liked it so much, that I adopted the metaphor as a way to help explain the world of investing to clients of Stone Consulting Group.

ANOTHER SAILING LESSON

My wife, Sabrina, and I enjoyed sailing, and during a vacation to Australia we decided to join a regatta in the Sydney Harbour. We spent the first hour being trained by a sailing expert before the race began. This was a fun race, not a serious competition, but the goal was to get through the course as fast as we could. All of the boats lined up, they blew the horn to start the race, and lo and behold, the wind completely stopped. In this sailing regatta, if you turned on your engine, you would be disqualified. All eight boats in the race sat and just drifted farther away from the finish line. We were naturally getting a little frustrated and thinking we were never going to make it through the course. Then far off in the distance, I saw a big oil tanker

6   As presented by Crestmont Research (www.CrestmontResearch.com)

heading into the harbor. I didn't really think much of it, because it was so far away. But the tanker continued to come closer to these eight little drifting sailboats. About twenty minutes later, it became apparent our little boats were going to be crushed by the tanker if we did not move. Unfortunately, we had to turn on our engines and get out of the way. If we didn't have an engine, you can bet we would have been rowing with oars with all of our energy because sometimes you need to do whatever is necessary to avoid disaster.

When investing, sometimes we can sail, and sometimes we need to row. Hopefully the following sailing and rowing metaphor will help explain a couple of different types of asset-allocation strategies. Back in the late 1980s, an influential study found that asset allocation, including market participation, is responsible for over 90 percent of the variance in portfolio performance.[7]

---

7   Gary P. Brinson, L. Randolph Hood, and Gilbert L. Beebower, "Determinants of Portfolio Performance," 1986, 1991 (follow-up study), *Financial Analysts Journal.*

ASSET ALLOCATION

Asset allocation is the decision of how to invest a pool of resources among broad asset classes. The purpose of asset allocation is to help control risk by reducing the volatility or degree of fluctuations of your portfolio and help to optimize your total return. This return on investment would include capital appreciation and interest or dividends. An optimized portfolio seeks to maximize the potential portfolio return for a given level of risk. In other words, a principal goal is to deliver the maximum level of return per unit of risk through diversification into several different asset classes.

So why allocate assets? Asset allocation has been identified as the single most important element of investment success. Research shows that 90 percent or more of a portfolio's return and risk is driven by asset allocation. The remaining 10 percent comes from other sources, such as security selection and active management. Investors who do not properly diversify may take higher risks in their portfolio but may not earn higher returns to compensate them for taking that risk.

Asset allocation provides three major benefits to an investor:

1. It provides a portfolio-management discipline, which will help the investor to avoid reacting to short-term market swings, emotions, and fads.

2. It emphasizes the development of an investment policy, an important factor for helping achieve investment return.

3. When followed over several market cycles, it reduces risk and volatility.

Asset allocation, however, is not a perfect solution. It cannot guarantee an investment will earn any given investment return. It is not as effective for short investment time horizons. It cannot eliminate all risks. It cannot guarantee a portfolio will never show a loss or have a losing year. It will not create a portfolio that will outperform a strong bull market. What it will do is provide you with a dedicated process to evaluate your investment management and determine if you are on schedule, or on course, to reach your destination in your journey of investing.

It is important to understand the two primary types of asset allocation: strategic and tactical.

A strategic asset-allocation model is, like sailing, one where you get in the investment sailboat and hang on. The market movement, whether it's up or down, will actively provide a rate of return directly in correlation with what happens in the market in which you are invested, whether it is in stocks or bonds, in the United States or internationally. This is often referred to as relative return. In other words, the return of your portfolio would be similar to the return of the major markets of which you are invested. To participate, we need to be invested in the market, much like you need to have your sails up to capture the wind. When there is no "financial wind," your account value will drift with the investment markets or investment "currents," so to speak.

Tactical asset allocation is more like being in a rowboat with a small sail, in which sometimes you can hoist up the sail and take advantage of the wind, but other times you will have to row to get where you need to go. There are also times when you will need to get out of harm's way. In those situations, you will be happy that you have the oars to help you row to safety. When the market nosedived in 2008 and the S&P 500[8] was down 37 percent, many tactical managers experienced a much different result. Most tactical money managers were down less than 10 percent, and a couple even had positive returns. However, when the US stock market rebounded from the Great Recession, the "financial wind" picked up and the strategic managers (the sailors) generally had better results than investors who were invested in the rowboats. A tactical manager might not provide the same type of upside, but they attempt to provide a substantial amount of downside protection. Of course, past performance does not guarantee future performance, and investment decisions should be made after you have identified your goals and how different types of investment plans can help you reach those goals.

Many types of asset-allocation options are familiar to most investors: cash, Treasury inflation-protected securities (TIPS), intermediate and long-term US bonds, high-yield corporate bonds, international bonds, real estate or real estate investment trusts, large-cap US stocks, small- and mid-cap US stocks, international stocks, emerging-market stocks, and emerging-market debt or bonds.

There are also asset-allocation options that are not correlated with market performance. Some of these might be considered alternative investments, and quite frankly, there is no assurance that the stated investment objectives really would be met. (See Appendix A for a full definition of an accredited investor.) But by having a diversified strategic asset-allocation model combined with a diversified tactical

---

8   The S&P 500 is an unmanaged index of stocks generally considered representative of the overall stock market.

asset-allocation model, we have found that our clients' success in meeting their goals and reaching their destination is enhanced.

The choice between strategic and tactical asset allocations in your portfolio should be determined not by your greed but by your need. Having a combination of tactical and strategic (rowing and sailing) asset allocation can be an effective way to reduce risk and provide you a way to help you reach your long-term financial objectives. The comprehensive financial-planning process you complete with your Personal CFO can help you evaluate and determine your need. The role that the Personal CFO plays is important to understand.

How an investment advisor or stockbroker handles their role with your investment plan will vary from advisor to advisor. Some want to make the day-to-day investment decisions. These brokers will do their own investment research and pick individual stocks and bonds, or they will use mutual funds as the preferred investment vehicle to create a portfolio for you. Others believe that while they could do a good job acting as the money manager for their clients, they feel that it is better to hire the best minds on Wall Street than try to compete with them. The Personal CFO's investment philosophy does not usually include constantly recommending different securities. If you are looking for an advisor to call you up on the phone and tell you that they have a great buy on Microsoft stock today, the Personal CFO is probably not right for you. Most do not consider themselves stock jockeys. However, if you want to have an advisor who will help you create and monitor your investment plan and coordinate that plan and its impact on the rest of your financial and business owner planning issues, the Personal CFO is probably a good fit. The Personal CFO does not usually have an incentive to keep you trading because their business is usually conducted for an advisory fee. Having your advisor paid on a fee basis means that as your investment accounts rise in value, so does the revenue received by the Personal CFO. That being said, though a Personal CFO may rarely be calling you with an investment idea, they will look for opportunities to help you to find investment solutions that are designed to improve the likelihood of your success within your financial and business plans.

A Personal CFO is not necessarily a money manager. They will actually help you find the money managers and monitor them. Money managers' jobs are pretty straightforward. The rules are set about how they should run a portfolio—is it stocks or bonds, is it domestic or international, can they use market timing or derivatives or margins, are they value or growth oriented, how much risk can they take, and so on. Then they just have one job, and given these restrictions, their job is to maximize the return.

A Personal CFO's job is very different from a money manager. Not only does the Personal CFO monitor these money managers, but he or she works with you to create the portfolio consisting of different managers and styles that match your needs as stated in your investment policy statement. The advisor's role is to be the client's advocate and to help that individual determine what he or she wants to accomplish. Then the focus should be to develop and maintain a plan that takes into account the resources and objectives that provides the highest probability of attaining their goals. Your success is not measured against artificial indices or standards but by one thing only—the question "Have your goals been met?"

INVESTMENT POLICY STATEMENTS

In my years of experience, I have come to understand the benefit of an investment policy statement. It is a statement designed to communicate the intent of the client regarding management of the portfolio and to provide a written strategy and standard that will guide the client in decisions regarding the management of investments. This statement should be reviewed at least annually and revisions made as necessary to reflect the changes in the client's circumstances or objectives. Historically, I have seen an investment policy statement directing the portfolio management for corporate pensions or university endowments. If it's good enough for the Stanford or Harvard University endowment, it should be good enough for my clients. Unfortunately, I have also found a large number of business owners who have a profit-sharing account for their company without an investment policy. This is especially important for those owners who are pooling their retirement plan assets with employees without any written policy for the investments.

The investment policy statement should include the following information:

> **Background**: An investment policy statement should include background information about the owner of the portfolio and make clear whether the assets are personal or business-use assets. The client is empowered to establish objectives, policies, and guidelines for the investment of the portfolio and the amount of assets covered by the investment policy. The client will select the investment options and may engage the services of investment advisors and planners who possess the qualifications and the ability to help provide prudent management of the portfolio. The last piece of background information is a listing of the specific accounts covered by this investment policy statement.

Objective: Next, the investment policy statement should address the client's investment objective and time horizon. Is the objective asset growth, income, preservation of capital, or a combination thereof? The client should identify the time frame to achieve the goal for this portfolio before meaningful withdrawals are expected to occur. For example, on our San Francisco Bay sailing trip through the Golden Gate, we needed to have an idea of how long it was going to take us. Would it take all day? Do we have two days or three days? If we needed to get it done in a couple hours and there was no wind, we never would have made it.

Remember the regatta in the Sydney Harbour where the timing got changed by external forces? Just as the approaching oil tanker changed the dynamics of that sailing adventure, external forces may change the dynamics of your investment journey. But the investment policy statement can help you monitor and identify how you can best accomplish the goals. It is important that the client provide adequate notice of any big life changes that may materially impact the implementation approach and/ or require all or part of the portfolio to be liquidated in order to meet those needs.

Risk Tolerance: The client's risk tolerance is based on attitude toward losses in their account. Including this information will help the Personal CFO know if the client is prepared to experience small, moderate, or large losses. Is the client willing to accept the risk necessary to achieve the investment objectives set forth in the investment policy statement? The overall portfolio investment results may be higher or lower, based on the client's stated tolerance and objectives.

Recommended Asset Allocation: After considering the client's investment objective, risk tolerance, and other related factors, the Personal CFO can recommend the initial asset allocation for the client to include minimum and maximum exposure to different asset classes.

Implementation and Products: The Personal CFO will work with the client to decide the type of portfolio used to implement the asset-allocation strategy, which may consist of individual securities, mutual funds, or other different types of investment vehicles. The client may engage the services of advisors and/or managers to help with the selection and oversight of the implementation strategy. That oversight should not become detached from the investment policy statement, because the products selected may need to be changed and updated over time to effectively implement the asset-allocation strategy.

Contributions and Liquidity: It is important to understand the client's liquidity needs and plans to make ongoing contributions. This will help the client and the advisor to fully understand how best to allocate the portfolio.

Client Service: Finally, the investment policy statement should reflect the Personal CFO's role in assisting the client with the oversight of the portfolio. The advisor should meet with the client on a mutually agreed schedule. The client should also inform the advisor of any changes in

goals or circumstances that may affect the management
of the portfolio.

As mentioned earlier, my experience has been that most individuals and business owners don't have an investment policy statement. In fact, many have not even heard of an investment policy statement. But this document is an important part of an investment plan and will help hold both the client and the advisor accountable to focus on their long-term goals and objectives. With this focus, the chances of success can be greater as you stay committed to your plan.

Having an investment policy statement has been a great benefit to my clients over the years. I have had situations where a client would call up and say something like, "Hey David, I had a great tip from a friend of mine on a stock, and I would like to invest a substantial sum in this stock because my friend said it's a sure thing." Of course, if we could all have a couple bucks for every sure thing we invested in or heard about, we'd all be really wealthy right now, wouldn't we? When I get a call like this from a client, I review their investment policy statement to determine if the purchase fits their goals and objectives.

I have a client who is a business owner who wanted to invest $100,000 of his retirement funds in a telecommunications company that his brother-in-law said was a sure thing. I expressed my concern—it was a penny stock—and showed him how it was contrary to his investment policy, but he insisted. I still advised him against the purchase, but since he was insistent, my client went ahead with the purchase. In the end, his $100,000 investment dropped to about $200.

In another situation, I had a client who had about 80 percent of his retirement funds in his own company's stock. When we first began his planning work, I explained how that was too high a concentration despite the company's remarkable performance. The stock had grown rapidly from around $10 a share up to $70 a share. The performance was so incredible that one of my client's fellow managers had 100 percent of his company retirement funds in the stock. Fortunately, my client took my advice to diversify his investment plan and sold it at $70 a share. Stock in the company, Lucent Technologies, kept rising to $74, until it plummeted to less than $5 a share when the tech bubble burst in 2002. Everybody had thought my client was crazy when he sold his stock at $70 a share, but it was a great decision based completely on the investment policy that was created during our first financial-planning engagement.

Typically when a client comes to me with a "sure thing," I will ask them if it meets with their investment objective. Some questions or statements your Personal CFO might say are, "This seems more risky than you were comfortable with when we were doing your investment policy statement," or "Where does this fit in your asset-allocation strategy we discussed six months ago?" The investment policy statement not only holds the advisor accountable but also keeps the client accountable to the goals.

That brings us back to implementing a strategy that focuses on the clients' needs instead of their greed. In your comprehensive financial plan, having your investment policy in place will help you and your advisor identify the timing, the risk tolerance, and the purposes for each investment that you have, along with your needs for liquidity. There are many different investment choices. This book, of course, won't make any specific investment recommendations (because such a generalized recommendation is the complete opposite approach to that of a Personal CFO). Let's review a few of the features of some of the most popular options.

DISCUSSION OF MUTUAL FUNDS

One of the most popular investment solutions is called a mutual fund. A mutual fund is a basket of individual securities managed professionally based on a particular set of investment guidelines. A mutual fund can invest in many different types of individual securities. Each mutual fund is very unique and can have a different set of objectives. These objectives are set out in what is called a prospectus. The prospectus will not only outline the investment objectives of the mutual fund, but will also explain charges and expenses associated with the fund. Mutual funds can be high in expense or relatively inexpensive. The expenses in mutual funds are referred as expense ratios and loads. You should always read the prospectus carefully before investing. A mutual fund is the product of an investment company whose role is to invest your assets and provide you investment management, much like the role of Intel is to make microchips or the role McDonald's is to make fast food. These investment companies or their products each may be focused on a specific asset class or strategy.

For example, if you want to invest in bonds, you can do so inside of a mutual fund. If you want to invest in stocks, whether it be US, international, small-cap or mid-cap, emerging-markets, or a real estate investment trust, you can invest in those inside of mutual funds. They have a very low minimum. A small investor can use mutual funds as a way to get into the investment marketplace. What types of mutual funds and how you invest in those funds really has to do with what makes the most sense for you and your situation.

Target-date funds are mutual funds that invest based on when you expect to need the money. For example, if you plan to retire in 2040, then you would choose a target 2040 fund with an investment mix that would become more conservative as 2040 approaches. Of course a target date fund is just that, a fund aiming for a particular a target or goal. Like any investment, there is no guarantee that the Target-date fund manager will 'hit the bullseye'.

Target-date funds also can be used in a 529 plan, which is a tax-advantaged way of saving for a beneficiary's higher education. Those long-term investment vehicles are obviously quite different from money-market funds, which are also mutual funds but invest in short-term government treasuries or corporate debt. A 529 plan also has offering documents like a prospectus that provide information about fees and expenses. It is always a good idea to review the offering documents since there are so many different options for investors.

The advantage of having mutual funds is it can give you the ability to have diversification even if you don't have a lot to invest. However, investors must be cautious about the costs and tax inefficiency of mutual funds.

Mutual funds are offered with different fee schedules, called loads. A load is a charge that compensates financial professionals who help clients invest their money. If you are a "do-it-yourselfer," you may want to purchase no-load mutual funds. You will be responsible for choosing the type of fund that you purchase. And since there are so many options, you'll find yourself trying to do your own research. Even within mutual funds, there are different classes of shares. Any financial professional should be happy to explain the differences.

ALTERNATIVES TO MUTUAL FUNDS

A concern I have using mutual funds for nonretirement money is tax inefficiency. If a fund manager invested in Microsoft in 1994 and has held that stock and watched it grow for many years, all of the mutual fund's shareholders would experience a large taxable gain from the fund selling those Microsoft shares. Even if you only owned shares in the mutual fund for a year, you would be affected.

An investment solution to consider is exchange-traded funds (ETFs). These are typically sector or industry specific and have lower expense ratios than mutual funds. ETFs are usually used in actively managed accounts. Of course, if you have enough assets to invest, the most cost-effective management is to purchase individual securities and to have a professional money manager manage those assets to fit your investment policy statement and your long-term financial objectives. In the past, most customized portfolios that use individual stocks and individual bonds required a minimum investment amount of $1,000,000. However, in the last year, a handful of professional money managers have made their customized portfolio solutions using individual securities available for as low as $100,000.

With smaller accounts, ETFs or mutual funds would be a more likely investment vehicle. These customized portfolios of individual stocks and bonds could provide a more tax-efficient alternative with limited or no mutual fund expense ratios. The elimination of an expense ratio on a mutual fund could save you an additional 1 percent off of your current management fees in addition to the likely increased tax efficiencies. Your Personal CFO can help direct you to these types of solutions if they fit with your personal investment goals and objectives.

When it comes to risk, my broker-dealer and Registered Investment Advisory (RIA) firm, Lincoln Financial Advisors, has done a very good job of describing their investment philosophy. This description of an investor's experience is in line with what I believe a client should experience. A national financial planning firm has stated in their firm philosophy that prudent investors should be adequately compensated for the risk that they assume.[9] They also believe that prudent investors should be positioned for a

---

9   Lincoln Financial Advisors, eLSPT Firm Philosophy, pg. 7.

reasonable probability of success relative to their goals and should not be exposed to potentially avoidable catastrophic risk. I believe that most investors would agree with that philosophy. How does a Personal CFO help implement this philosophy to provide a client with a predictable experience?

INVESTMENT PROCESS: A CONTINUUM

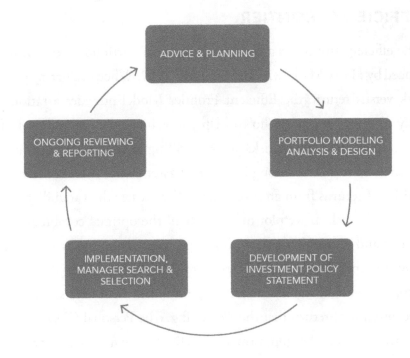

Bringing an investor philosophy like this to life is done with a focus on professional advice, consulting, and planning. It's also done through portfolio modeling analysis and design, along with the development of your investment policy statement. Searching for and selecting a manager specifically able to implement your investment policy statement is followed up with ongoing monitoring and due diligence. This type of investment planning process integrates asset allocation, active management, and tax management in a way that seeks to reduce uncompensated risks, capture manager skill, and help reduce the impact of taxes to help enhance the client's net total return over time. The process of comprehensive financial planning with a professional who acts like your Personal CFO will help you better understand where you are with regard to not only your investment goals but the rest of your planning goals as well.

EFFICIENT FRONTIER

The efficient frontier is a concept in modern portfolio theory introduced by Harry Markowitz and others in 1952. When evaluating your risk versus return, the Efficient Frontier Model provides a rational way to diversify a portfolio to help you achieve the highest level of potential return for the risks you are willing to take. Significant differences in risk exist among investment asset classes. Risk is the variability of returns from an investment. The greater the variability, the greater the risk. If we plot on a graph all the optimal combinations of risk and return that a portfolio could have, it appears as a curving upward line. That's the Efficient Frontier, but most of the time, people are below the line and taking more risk than they should for the amount of return that they're getting. The Personal CFO should use the model to develop ways for the client to be more efficient with the amount of risk that they are taking. Do you know where your portfolio is as it relates to risk and return on the Efficient Frontier? The following graphic is a sample portfolio sorted by asset class, with the model of an "efficient frontier" represented by the curve. The Equity Style box refers to a common way to classify stocks and investments by their size and objective.

EFFICIENT FRONTIER MODEL

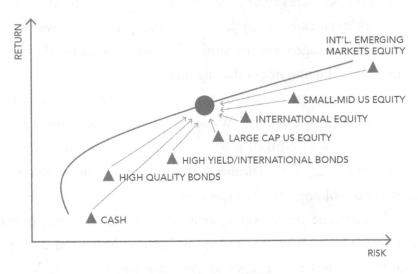

EQUITY STYLE BOX

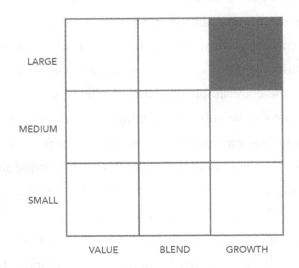

INVESTMENT STYLES

Another useful theory has to do with the style of your investment management: value, growth, or a blend of the two. A shopping analogy can help explain the differences between how a value investment manager would invest your money compared with a growth investment manager. You might go shopping at Walmart for convenience because there's a variety of merchandise in one location. But the overriding reason you go there is low prices. That is the way value investment managers are investing. They are looking for the great deals. They're buying stocks that are undervalued.

An often-quoted piece of investment advice is: "Buy when there's blood in the streets." Whoever first said this, supposedly a nineteenth-century banker, had the objective of purchasing investments when they were cheapest. That's what a value investment manager is looking for—the great deals.

To continue the shopping analogy, a growth manager is like someone who goes to Nordstrom or Neiman Marcus and is less concerned with the price tags and more concerned about the service and the quality of goods. In fact, a growth manager is focused on factors such as the momentum of an industry or the strength and financials of a company. Most of all, the growth manager is looking for an opportunity for the stocks to bring capital appreciation.

Of course, there are shoppers in the middle, who go to Macy's department stores, maybe only buying things when they're on sale. A blend of the value and growth investment management styles is like that Macy's sale. The investment manager is looking for value and the qualities that will lead to growth. Some people refer to this investment style as GARP, or growth at a reasonable price.

Those two primary styles of equity investing, growth and value, both offer a disciplined approach for potential capital appreciation, but each considers the selection of stocks in a fundamentally different way. So, value investing identifies stocks that are currently selling for less than their perceived worth. They are often mature dividend-paying companies and cyclical businesses, meaning their prospects may be significantly influenced by the course of the overall economy.

Growth investing targets stocks of companies with rising earnings that are often developing new products or services or expanding into a new market. Because these stocks are selected for their future growth potential, they may have high prices relative to the current earnings and generally pay a low dividend, if any. Depending on market conditions, these two styles perform differently. However, by including both in an investment program, you can potentially reduce the risk while positioning the portfolio to take advantage of opportunities under a variety of different economic climates.

Performance by investment style can vary dramatically. A well-diversified portfolio assures participation in the styles that are performing well and facilitates staying the course. Like on our "strategic sailboat," trying to stay the course is sometimes hard. But staying the course may help you achieve your objective more so than chasing the most recent best performer. Diversification is a method used to manage risk, but it does not eliminate risk, guarantee a profitable investment return, or guarantee against a loss.

All of this information may overwhelm you. The Personal CFO's goal is to offer objective, strategic advice. Your advisor should be in the center of the Financial-Planning Wheel of Fortune to provide you and your family prudent direction that will put you closer not only to the investment objectives that you have for your family or business but also to the other financial goals you have established as part of your plan.

Whomever you go to for advice, I would recommend that you have that advisor help you create an investment policy statement. The focus should be on the financial plan and working toward accomplishing those objectives that will bring you the most peace and financial satisfaction.

CHAPTER 5

REAL ESTATE AND RELUCTANT LANDLORDS

Real estate is in my blood. My family has been in the real estate business since the early 1960s. At the encouragement of my father and older brother Ron, who is a Certified Property Manager®, I decided to study and take the appropriate classes and exams to receive my California real estate agent's license in 1991. This additional study and years of industry experience has helped me to provide advice for our clients. It also helps me appreciate and understand the advantages as well as the limitations of different real estate solutions.

As discussed in chapter 4, many different asset classes can provide investment diversification. One of those asset classes is ownership in real estate. Direct ownership, such as buying a primary residence, often with a mortgage, is the most common. There are multiple ways to invest in real estate, some allowing you to sit back and collect income without all the headaches of being a landlord. There also are different ways to hold title, which is important because it will determine how you and your heirs will benefit from the real estate, whether your objective is to have income or capital appreciation in the value of your property or a combination of the two.

Some ways to invest in real estate include ownership in real estate partnerships as a limited partner or a general partner, even using family limited partnerships. You can own real estate, or fractional interests in real estate, through your participation in an LLC (limited liability company). A real estate investor can also use incorporation to own real estate in an attempt to limit exposure to the potential liabilities inherent in this asset class. You can own real estate in traded or nontraded real estate investment trusts, called REITs. You can own it as a tenant in common or even own beneficial interests in Delaware Statutory Trusts.

Understanding your objective in owning the real estate will help you determine which of these types of investments are most appropriate for your situation. A Personal CFO can assist you in creating a strategy of owning your real estate for the specific needs that you have in your personal situation.

There are seven primary real estate asset types:

- single-family homes

- multifamily residences, including apartment complexes, condominiums, duplexes, and mobile home parks.

- retail—ranging from single-tenant stores to malls, outdoor shopping centers, and the power centers anchored by big-box stores

- offices—whether in suburbia, in central business districts downtown, or in between (Investing in office real estate can be tricky; having multiple tenants or a single tenant changes the dynamic of your investment.)

- industrial real estate, which includes manufacturing, warehouses, and distribution centers

- hospitality or hotels, motels, and resorts

- raw land or agricultural real estate

REITS

Real estate is typically a fairly nonliquid asset and often lacks diversification. Most real estate investors own the same types of properties in similar geographic regions. This lack of diversification may be by accident or by design for ease of management. Those seeking a more liquid alternative can buy into a real estate investment trust, or REIT. This can be accomplished by purchasing shares of common stock in a REIT or owning a REIT mutual fund. These are liquid securities and can be traded on the stock exchanges. They are invested in real estate properties but have similar volatility to that of small- or mid-cap value stocks.

Not all REITs are traded that way. When you purchase a nontraded REIT, you are investing in a portfolio of real estate that is not traded on any stock exchange. A nontraded REIT is a nonliquid investment, and each investor should expect to own shares in that investment program for many years. Typically, a nontraded REIT would take anywhere from three to ten years or longer before it has a liquidation event. A liquidation event is typically called "going full cycle." This full-cycle event usually creates liquidity for investors as I described below. Sometimes these events involve a REIT being listed on a stock exchange or merging with another, traded REIT. This means your nontraded REIT is now a traded REIT and is now a stock as described earlier.

Another full-cycle or liquidation event could involve a nontraded REIT being purchased by another investment entity for cash. Large investment programs usually have a certain amount of real estate that they desire in their portfolio allocation. Since REITs are typically significant in size, this becomes an efficient way for a large foundation, a university endowment, or a corporate pension plan to increase their allocation to real estate in their portfolio. When a large investor like this buys these big portfolios of real estate at a specific price, the REIT shareholders receive proceeds from the sale of the real estate. At that time, the investor will receive the cash proceeds from the sale, and then each investor will individually determine what they will do with the proceeds. Going full cycle is usually a good thing for an investor, providing flexibility and liquidity. The only negative could be capital gains taxes if there is a gain on the sale of the real estate. Not all REITs are created equal, so you have to be careful with this type of real estate investing and do your research. In the end, make sure you know what you are getting into, and educate yourself on the REIT purchase you are considering.

1031 EXCHANGES

I recently assisted a client in a like-kind real estate exchange of an office park for another real estate asset. This is called a 1031 exchange. The IRS code 1031 offers investors an opportunity to transfer ownership from one real estate property to another and defer the capital gains tax on the sale. That's an important and sophisticated strategy move.

For example, if you had purchased a piece of property for $1 million ten years ago and sold that property today for $2 million, then you would be recognizing a taxable capital gain of $1 million or more if you depreciated your property over the prior ten years for tax-deduction purposes. IRS code 1031 provides investors the opportunity to invest proceeds of their sale into another qualifying piece of real estate to defer the taxes and continue to receive the benefit of real estate ownership.

There are some rules you must follow when completing a 1031 exchange. In a like-kind real estate exchange, the first thing you must do is work closely with your real estate professional to make sure the proper language is in the sales contract to take full advantage of the tax deferral. Second, you must identify a qualified intermediary. This company will hold the cash from the sale proceeds until you are ready to close escrow on the replacement property. Once you have closed escrow on the sale, you have forty-five days in which to identify your replacement property and 180 days to close escrow on that new property. If you are unable to meet these deadlines, the transactions will not qualify as a 1031 exchange, and you will recognize the capital gains and owe the taxes.

Also, if you have debt on your current property that you are exchanging, you need to replace that debt dollar for dollar. For example, if you are selling a property for $1 million that has a $400,000 mortgage, you will be required to buy a property worth at least $1 million with at least a $400,000 mortgage. Failing to meet that requirement would create boot or mortgage boot. If you bought another property for $1 million with only $300,000 worth of mortgage, the $100,000 mortgage boot would be a taxable capital gain assuming you made at least $100,000 on the sale. If you do not have any debt on your current property, then it is less complicated.

HOW TO HOLD TITLE

Expert help also is important in deciding how to hold title on real estate investments. For example, property acquired by a couple during marriage is defined as community property in some state laws. Decisions on how to hold title should be coordinated with your Personal CFO along with your attorney and CPA. There are income tax ramifications in how you own your real estate or any other investment. IRS rules cover how capital gains are determined if a spouse passes away and is on title. In one case, if a spouse passes away, the taxpayer is eligible to potentially have a step up in the cost basis to the value of the property at the date of death or six months post death instead of the value when they bought the original real estate property twenty or thirty years prior.

One client, Harold, sold a residential rental property in California he'd purchased in the 1960s for a nice profit. Prior to closing escrow, he decided, with the help of his Personal CFO, that a 1031 exchange would be appropriate for him and would fit with his income needs in his financial plan. This tax-deferred exchange was for an investment into a property located in Washington State. The new property had a long-term lease with a national retailer and provided him very good cash flow for many years. When Harold died, he passed his beneficial interest in the property to his heirs. The ownership was appropriately split by the heirs, and they were able to continue to collect the cash flow from the Washington retail property. A few years after Harold's death, the real estate manager of the property determined the timing was right to sell the real estate to another investor. Due to IRS rules, the heirs were able to sell the real estate post death with a smaller capital gain than if they had been gifted the real estate prior to Harold's death. The proceeds were taxed based on the higher-cost basis value of the property, not the client's original purchase price in the 1960s. This saved Harold's heirs, then in their fifties and sixties, a lot of income taxes. How do you hold title?

Mark Jackson and his business partners had owned two office parks for many years, each with a mortgage that represented about 50 percent of the property's value. The business partners were concerned about the best way to pass the properties on to the individual family members when each of the business partners died. Mark's Personal

CFO assisted him in completing a 1031 exchange. In the process, Mark's advisors had to make sure that the debt was replaced in the exchange so that he could defer all of the capital gains from the sales of these two office parks. Working in coordination with the client's CPA, they chose to use a Delaware Statutory Trust (DST) to accomplish their goal. The DST simplified the day-to-day real estate management operations for Mark and provided a more predictable cash flow for him and his wife as well as his business partners and their spouses. What he also gained in the exchange was increased real estate portfolio diversification. This was accomplished by going from owning two office parks in the same community to having interests in four different multifamily residential properties in two different states. In addition, like Harold in the previous example, the DST structure provided Mark and his business partners an easy way to have the ownership in the real estate properties be equally distributed between their children at their deaths. This DST ownership strategy will help the investors' estates to easily distribute income or future real estate sales proceeds to each of the partners' heirs without conflicts between surviving business partners and Mark's children.

BECOMING HOME DEPOT'S LANDLORD

Another client, Gene Johnson, inherited a piece of raw land many years ago in his hometown. He received no income from the raw land but was obligated to pay the property taxes. At the recommendation of his Personal CFO, Gene decided to sell the land and diversify his real estate portfolio. This transaction was also done in a Delaware Statutory Trust, and after shopping around for opportunities around the country, Gene became the proud owner of a beneficial interest in a retail property leased by Walgreens in Salt Lake City, Utah. He and his wife, Margaret, received income from this property of about

$1,000 a month for over ten years. That's more than $120,000, but it's only the beginning of the story. When the Walgreens store was subsequently sold to another investor, Gene worked with his Personal CFO for recommendations. He considered taking the cash proceeds and just paying the taxes. However, after reviewing the tax implications, Gene decided to complete a second 1031 exchange. He and his Personal CFO considered various properties, including a medical office building in Chicago and apartment complexes in Florida, Colorado, and Texas. Gene liked the idea of a single company with long-term leases rather than multiple small-tenant leases. Once again, Gene used a Delaware Statutory Trust structure. This time, the DST owned properties occupied by two Home Depot stores, one in Washington State and the other in Massachusetts. This provided Gene and Margaret additional regional diversification for their real estate portfolio, which also included residential properties in California. The Johnsons are currently receiving more income from the Home Depot stores than they were receiving from the DST that owned the Salt Lake City property. If they were still sitting on that original raw land, they would have no income from their real estate, having nothing but a piece of dirt and over ten years of property tax bills. Owning income producing real estate can help create a valuable income stream for investors.

DIVERSIFICATION FOR THE RELUCTANT LANDLORD

Owning a piece of dirt and just paying taxes on it, as Gene once did, can be frustrating if you are looking for income. Having tenants can be even more of a headache, and that is often the motivation for clients to seek more passive real estate investments. But there is another reason to do so. Diversification is a basic part of investment planning and should be incorporated into real estate portfolios, as the clients did in the two previous examples. Unfortunately, it is common for real estate investors to have all of their holdings in the same region or of the same asset type. Even those who desire some diversification might not know where to begin looking or how to use strategies such as the 1031 exchange and a Delaware Statutory Trust to control capital gains taxes and provide additional benefits to the investors and their families as illustrated in some of the prior examples. While a DST can be a good income-producing asset, it is only for accredited investors (see Appendix A) and is inappropriate for investors who are not prepared to hold a nonliquid asset for an extended period of time, probably seven to ten years or longer.

Those considering real estate investments should seek help from an expert who has assisted other individuals in navigating the complexities. DSTs represent just one of various types of ownership available in real estate. When you own real estate, it's also important to consider asset-protection strategies. If one of your tenants, or a customer of one of your tenants, has an accident and sues, what is your liability? If you are a limited partner and have limited exposure, then you will not be putting anything more at risk than the real estate you own in that partnership. Decisions that you and your Personal CFO make regarding asset protection should be coordinated with your attorney and CPA.

IS REAL ESTATE AN ALTERNATIVE INVESTMENT?

Most Personal CFOs consider real estate to be in the same "alternative investment" class as investments like oil and gas partnerships, managed futures strategies, hedge funds, and absolute return strategies. Alternative investments are not for everyone, but these unique solutions help provide diversification for an investor. Generally speaking, more diversification helps reduce the overall volatility of an investment portfolio. The correlation between alternative investments and more common asset classes like US stocks is usually less than between US and international stocks, creating greater diversity.

Your Personal CFO should assist you by identifying what alternative investment programs might best fit your individual situation. In addition, your advisor's broker-dealer should complete a thorough review of each program it makes available to investors. This review is done to protect investors, their advisors, and the broker-dealer. This due-diligence process and the completion of additional education for your advisor is highly recommended before you decide to add an alternative investment program to your portfolio.

There are many real estate companies that offer different investment programs for accredited and nonaccredited investors. If a thorough due-diligence process is done correctly, not all programs will pass inspection. There are a number of reasons why a particular program might be denied. Some might involve the elevated risks in the details of a commercial lease or poor terms of the financing attached to a property. Other reasons for denial might involve excessive fees, limited cash flows, or increased risks with limited upside potential. However, some broker-dealers base their approval decisions exclusively on the basis of the organization offering the program. While the company's history and reputation should be important, it should not be the exclusive reason for approval of a product.

How should real estate or economic cycles affect your investment decisions? During the great recession of 2007 through 2009, office real estate properties in central business districts (CBDs) saw significant reductions in property values. The economic downturn really beat up financial companies, and it showed in their reduced need for office space along with many other corporate tenants in

CBDs in places like New York, Chicago, and San Francisco. Office real estate had also been hurt as more people began to telecommute. Short-term leases negatively affected cash flows received by real estate investors, while tenants reduced their square footage and created a rise in vacancies in CBDs across the nation. Real estate investors who had a more diversified portfolio that included properties with long-term leases had a more stable cash flow during this difficult time. Long-term retail leases like grocery stores, or other necessity retail like drugstores, help you deal with bubbles and busts in the real estate market. These retail investments may have a lease that's twenty years long, allowing you to ride out economic cycles as long as the particular company leasing the space stays in business. Of course, there are pros and cons to different types of real estate, and there really is no solution that would be considered one size fits all. That being said, some real estate investors do like properties that have long-term triple net leases. In a triple net lease, the tenant is responsible for paying insurance premiums, property taxes, and upkeep on the building. That helps create a more stable income or cash flow for the investor.

When real estate income is received, it's usually more tax efficient than other dividend-like investments because the investor can recognize tax deductions due to depreciation from the ownership of the improvements on the property.

Once you start considering all of the different dynamics of investing in real estate, you really need to have someone help you do it right. Like any investment, your Personal CFO should be able to assist you in determining which types of real estate investments make sense for you. That's also true of retirement planning, which we discuss in the next chapter.

CHAPTER 6

A NEW WAY OF MAKING RETIREMENT MORE REWARDING

From 1983 to 1985, I served as a missionary in South Africa. It was an amazing experience for a twenty-year-old to be focused for a couple years on service to other people. This experience helped shape me as a young man and gave me conviction about how great joy can be received while serving others.

I met many wonderful people while I was there. One of those individuals was a man by the name of Winston Langlois. Like me, Winston was a missionary focused on helping the people in South Africa. But unlike me, he was a senior citizen, serving with his always-smiling wife, Alice. They arrived in Cape Town in 1984 when Winston was about seventy years old. I assumed he was retired. Winston, a short man with a mustache and a cheerful voice and manner, was an attorney and had passed the California bar in 1940. As of 1984, Winston had been practicing law for over forty years.

I left South Africa in 1985, but Winston and Alice stayed on to serve until 1986. After my mission, I attended Brigham Young University, met my sweetheart, Sabrina, got married, had a couple kids, moved to the Sacramento area, and attended MBA school.

Then I began my financial-planning practice in 1992, had a couple more kids, and quite frankly had forgotten about Winston and Alice Langlois and our friendship until the late 1990s. One day I was visiting a local estate-planning attorney in Sacramento. Leaving his office, I looked into a window of another law office and saw Winston. He was sitting there working in an office. I immediately went in to see my old friend. He was well into his eighties and was continuing to practice law. Financially, he didn't need to work. He did it because he enjoyed serving others and loved studying the law. I saw him for many years following, sitting in his law office as I would pass by on the way to meetings. I believe he worked into his early nineties until he passed away in 2010.

Winston and Alice Langlois and David Stone in Cape Town, South Africa

So what does this story have to do with retirement planning? In 2001, I was introduced to a book called *The New Retirementality* by Mitch Anthony. Over fifteen years ago, as I read the chapter "You're

Only Old When You Think You Are," I wrote the name of Winston Langlois in the margin. I ran across that notation recently, and it made me smile. Anthony's premise in the book is that times have changed since the day when people would retire at sixty-five, get the gold watch and company pension, and sit on the front porch all day just watching people walk by.

When I first read Anthony's book, I had my own vision of my retirement at age sixty. Maybe I would not get a gold watch, but I planned to retire and just take time to relax. Later I came to the conclusion that I wanted to follow in Winston's footsteps and take time off to serve others and later return to working with my clients. In fact, my retirement plan now says seventy, but who knows? My father, for example, at eighty-eight years old, still goes into the office three days a week. Hey, if my mind is sharp, let's keep it going.

FINANCIAL INDEPENDENCE

In working with different clients over the years, I find that they have some hard and fast goals regarding their retirement or financial independence. We may choose to stop working or choose to work longer. What do we want our retirement to look like? How do we visualize our golden years? Those questions affect how we know when we are or will be financially independent. Quantifying financial independence, or the point at which you have accumulated sufficient resources to provide for yourself throughout your life, is a key element in developing a plan that will allow you to not only consider more traditional family needs but a much broader range of issues as well.

Most people are actively saving and investing with the goal of eventually being able to independently support their expenses for life. In my experience, I've found that most people don't plan to run their checking account down to zero on the day they die but in fact continue to grow their estates over their lifetime. However, understanding your particular time frame for financial independence will dictate how you manage your resources to provide not only for college education or retirement but also for generational family wealth or a charitable legacy.

So, do you feel that you're on track for your financial independence? Do you know if you're saving enough for retirement? Do you know if it will be sufficient for you to meet your goals? Do you even have goals? A Personal CFO should be able to help you establish goals if you don't have any. I love that a Personal CFO can help his or her clients with these questions so that they truly understand where they stand financially based on their current actions and lifestyle, and when they will be financially independent. This is all part of the Personal CFO's process. Knowing if and when a client is able to experience financial independence is a critical part in helping most clients to appreciate and experience the Power of a Plan—their personal, customized plan dedicated to providing them knowledge. Knowledge is power, and there is power in a plan.

EXPENSE CATEGORY BREAKDOWN

In 1994, another Certified Financial Planner™, Briggs Matsko, invited me to be part of a meeting with one of his clients—Dean, a physician. Since that meeting, Briggs and I have worked with Dean and his wife, Carol Ann, for many years. At first, the focus of our planning was on the accumulation of assets to build toward their personal financial independence. As Dean got closer to retirement, Briggs and I realized that we had been so focused early on helping people grow their wealth that we had not come up with the most creative ways to help clients create their retirement distribution plans. Retirement planning is really figuring out how much wealth you need to accumulate for retirement, and retirement distribution planning is the organization and determination of the most efficient solutions to provide cash flow for the client during their retirement years. Through the process of working with Dean and Carol Ann, Briggs and I worked together to establish a simple system that breaks down different types of retirement income needed for the client. Briggs went on to make retirement distribution planning an emphasis of his business and having worked with him for many years, I for one really appreciate his expertise in this area.

His planning experience with Dean and Carol Ann eventually led to the creation of the "E.A.S.E." process. This process was established by Briggs and his associates at Retirement Security Centers and involves helping the client *envision* different income categories and needs during retirement. Next, the E.A.S.E. process involves *analysis* to determine the impact of different planning scenarios on a client's retirement. Then *solutions* are provided, which include different product alternatives and life decisions to help the clients optimize their success and create the best sources to fund those needs. Finally, an *evaluation* is performed regularly to make sure the clients are on track and to adjust for changes in their situation. A Personal CFO would use a similar process to help you create a financial roadmap for you and your family.

As you can see from the chart on the next page, your retirement income needs or desires are broken into three categories:

- **Core expenses** are things like food, clothing, housing, transportation, insurance, and taxes. We want these expenses to be covered by income sources that are reliable, like an employer pension or Social Security benefits, or perhaps a personal pension annuity. This will then provide you and your family a consistent monthly cash flow to take care of the basics of life, your core living expenses.

- **Joy expenses** include things like travel, hobbies or entertainment, and even gifts to family and friends. Your joy expenses are funded from dividends from your investments or earnings, interest, or the sale of assets from existing securities or real estate that you own.

- The desire to leave a legacy is the wealth transfer you leave for your heirs and/or charity. That essentially is what's left over once you and your spouse pass away.

RETIREMENT INCOME MATRIX

SOURCE: RETIREMENT SECURITY CENTERS
© 2004, 2006, 2013 RETIREMENT SECURITY CENTERS. ALL RIGHTS RESERVED.

Breaking these expenses into different categories helps you and the Personal CFO establish how you're going to fund different retirement income needs, and at the same time, work closely with your accountant on tax-efficiency issues. Briggs and I used this approach to help Dean and Carol Ann understand how their financial resources would be used to best serve their cash flow needs. We took the time to listen and understand their core expenses. Whenever I talk with clients about their core and joy expenses, I find it interesting because it's such a reflection of personal opinions and values.

I recently had a conversation about expenses with another client, who happens to be a CERTIFIED FINANCIAL PLANNER™ Professional, herself. Most of her core expenses were things I probably would have categorized as joy expenses. For example, driving a Mercedes is not really a core expense. I teased her about it, and we laughed, but in reality, it's her decision. So in the end, we focus on building the income to provide for those core expenses, Mercedes or Chevrolet.

At the same time, your Personal CFO should look at the tax strategies element of how those particular needs are met. I'd like to share an illustration of what I call The Three Boxes. These three boxes help us to discuss the basics of retirement planning.

RETIREMENT-PLANNING BASICS

There are three basic ways that we can defer or avoid paying income taxes when it comes to saving or investing for retirement. We can **deduct** dollars from our earned income. We can **grow** the values from that income on a tax-deferred basis, or we can take an **income** from an account on a tax-free basis.

Unfortunately, the IRS will never let us have all three boxes. The best we can hope for is two out of three.

RETIREMENT-PLANNING BASICS

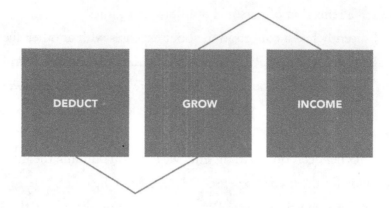

When we put money into the **deduct** and **grow** boxes, we pay no taxes when we make our contribution. However, when we draw the money out of these two boxes, the dollars are taxed as ordinary income based on our tax rate at that time.

RETIREMENT-PLANNING BASICS

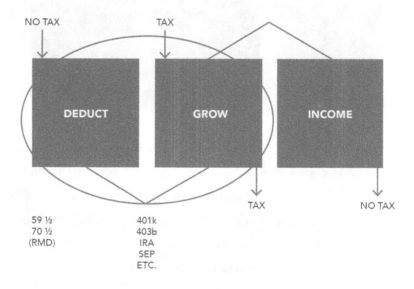

As you can see, some examples of these types of tax-deferred retirement plans are the 401(k) for corporate employees, 403(b) for not-for-profits, the IRA (individual retirement account), and the SEP (simplified employee pension). I like to refer to these as government restricted plans. There are limitations on how much you can contribute to a 401(k) plan or a 403(b) plan. There are waiting periods before you can take distributions from these plans without a government penalty, such as age fifty-nine and a half for the 401(k). By seventy and a half, you're required to take minimum distributions from these types of plans.

Now let's talk about the **grow** and **income** boxes.

RETIREMENT-PLANNING BASICS

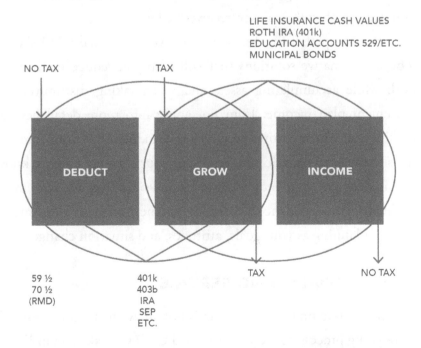

With these two boxes, you pay taxes on income now, and then when you pull money from these accounts you pay no taxes. Just like the government restricted plans on the left, the **grow** and take **income** boxes have rules you must abide by.

Can you think of any types of accounts or plans where you can save, invest, or get these types of tax benefits on the **grow** and take **income** side? There are four basic types of accounts:

- municipal bonds

- educational accounts such as 529 plans or Coverdell or education IRAs

- the Roth IRA or Roth 401(k)

- life insurance cash values

Of course, like the **deduct** and **grow** boxes where there are limitations, the same thing is true with the **grow** and take **income** boxes. You need to obey the rules to receive the benefits.

In a comprehensive financial plan, your Personal CFO should look at alternative solutions that will help you reduce tax liability both while accumulating assets and when taking distribution of retirement plan income. I am not going into more detail here or making recommendations, because just as in the rest of your comprehensive financial plan, it is necessary for your Personal CFO to know and understand your individual goals and objectives for retirement or financial independence. Over time, you need to make adjustments in your planning as your goals, attitudes, and situation changes.

NEEDS, GOALS, AND SERVICE

Comprehensive financial planning is not an event. It's a process. It's an ongoing process where your Personal CFO will take a snapshot in time to see what's changed in your life. Your needs will change. Your health will change. Income tax rates and income tax laws will change.

Your rate of return will change from day to day, month to month, and year to year. In the end, it's important that you have an ongoing process to be able to experience the power of your plan.

I began this chapter with a story from my service as a missionary in Africa in the 1980s, an experience that gave me a passion for serving people. When I interview clients who have had service experiences in their lives, such as the armed services or Peace Corps, I ask them about their experience. Their answer helps me understand the types of things for which they would like to be remembered. I have found that people who have experienced high levels of participation in compassionate service usually desire to ensure that their families can have the same types of experiences. I see my business as a financial mission where I'm helping my clients reach their financial objectives, their dreams, and their hopes. Your life experiences have shaped who you are and where you want to leave your legacy.

I remember a story from the book *The New Retirementality* that helped me review my personal priorities. A father once said that his daughter asked him to come out and play. He said, "No, Honey, Dad's too busy." His daughter said, "You're always too busy," and went out to play. That night he kept turning it over in his head, "Why do I work so hard?" Answer: to get freedom. Why do I want freedom? Answer: to spend time with those I love. When am I going to have this freedom or make getting it a priority? Answer: probably about the time my kids are gone. He realized that he had put himself in a vicious cycle of motion and money and had everything turned upside down.

That story says a lot about why it's important for people to take the time when they're young and healthy to be with their family. I want clients to have that "new retirementality"—that is, to be able to focus on taking the time to provide service to others and to do things with their children or grandchildren now. I'm a soccer coach. I've helped with my sons' Boy Scout troops. I've been involved in my church, in my community, in industry organizations. I do those things because, like my father, I plan on working much longer than sixty-five years old.

My wife and I plan to serve a mission like Alice and Winston Langlois did. In fact, we plan to serve multiple missions. There will be other associates in our firm who will be here to work with our clients while I'm gone for a year or so. Then I will come back and work some more and go serve again, and then come back and work some more. That is the long-term plan for Stone Consulting Group, as I have great team members here who can assist my clients while I am off serving people overseas. I plan to do that while I'm younger because my intent is to be able to spend time doing the things that will provide me and my family joy as well as helping others. It is the type of legacy I personally want to leave for my family and my clients as I encourage them to get involved and to serve in their communities and in the areas where they feel they have a passion.

INVESTING FOR SERVICE

Making a plan of how you can prepare financially to serve others brings us back to the three boxes and the distinction between tax-deferred retirement plans, with their rules about when you can take out the money. As you plan to create a strategy how best to receive income while taking time away from work, your Personal CFO will be able to assist you in making a plan that best suits your specific dreams. There are many different alternative ways for you to prepare financially for that service experience. Each of those ways will have different tax implications, depending on which of the three boxes you are using. Business owners in particular have the ability to create deferred compensation plans for themselves or their key employees. In my nonqualified deferred compensation plan, I have chosen to have funds start coming out at a time geared toward my plans to serve a mission. Similarly, if I have a client who wants to do something like a mission or sabbatical when they're in their fifties, then I wouldn't want them to have to use tax-deferred retirement funds and pay a penalty for early withdrawal. Your Personal CFO just needs to identify what works best for you based on your specific plan or vision for your future.

Retirement planning is only one of many areas where tax strategy is important. We discuss others in the next chapter.

CHAPTER 7

TAX STRATEGIES FOR THE LONG-FORM CROWD

Things happen for a reason. Over ten years ago, our firm received a call from a CPA who was trying to figure out how to best assist a client who wanted to hold real estate in a retirement account. He reached the receptionist, who eventually asked me if I would be willing to answer a quick question from a CPA about a real estate topic. I had maintained a real estate license since 1991, so she felt I might be the best person to answer his question. I took the call and met Bill, a CPA located in northern Nevada. We discussed his question and determined that his call to my office was accidental. He was trying to reach a completely different company. The funny thing was that even after we discovered the error, we ended up chatting for over an hour. Based on our discussion, he was interested in learning more about our firm. Eventually he joined Lincoln Financial Advisors' CPA program called SolutionsLinc. This program was established to provide CPAs a way to create a strategic alliance with professional financial-planning-oriented advisors who are committed to the planning process. This particular CPA not only became a part of the SolutionsLinc partnership with Stone Consulting Group, but he and his wife also became a client of our firm.

Of course, it doesn't always happen that quickly. In another circumstance, I was hired by a physician who, with our help in collaboration with her CPA, Dennis, created a medical group. After working together for over fifteen years, Dennis and I decided that we should go to lunch. During that lunch, we discussed his determination to do better with his own personal and business owner planning. I had the honor to meet his wife and ultimately help them get their financial house in order in the areas of estate planning by introducing him to an estate-planning attorney, as well as assisting him and his family and his employees with their risk management, retirement planning, investment planning, cash management, and so on. During our many meetings, we even came up with some interesting tax-planning ideas.

I have found that with tax planning, like other areas of life, unless you have someone helping you choose what questions to ask, sometimes you miss out on opportunities. People's relationships with their CPAs vary a lot. Some CPAs are trusted advisors who provide creative tax-planning ideas. Others are more like historians writing a report by examining documents and then sending it on to the federal and state income tax agencies.

I share these stories with you because I truly believe that collaborating with my clients' CPAs helps those clients make better decisions. Tax professionals who collaborate with an advisor like a Personal CFO also believe in the Power of a Plan. Together they implement tax strategies that help their clients be more tax efficient in their financial and business owner planning.

The types of areas you would want your Personal CFO to collaborate with your accountant would include tax efficiency in investments, tax deferral in benefits, and strategies for deductions, to name a few. The following is a review of some of these areas.

TAX EFFICIENCY IN INVESTMENTS

How much of your taxable accounts are invested in mutual funds? KPMG, a major accounting firm, did a study several years ago that found that the difference in rate of return between the average mutual fund and tax-efficient mutual funds was about 1.5 percent.[10] If an investment offers a tax efficiency that could help save about 1.5 percent, that could be the difference of $15,000 on a $1 million portfolio. While that may not sound like much, over a twenty-year period on a portfolio earning roughly 7 percent annually, the difference through compounding may be as much as, if not more than, the original value of the portfolio itself, or $1 million.

It is not unusual for investors to be surprised or disappointed by the impact of taxes on their portfolio and also be unsure whether they can do anything about it. A Personal CFO's approach is to collaborate with your tax advisor in designing your portfolio to maximize your after-tax wealth.

Here are some questions to ponder:

- Is anyone actively managing my portfolio to take advantage of the opportunities to reduce taxes that arise periodically?

- How did I determine which investments should be held in my tax-deferred versus my currently taxable accounts?

- Do I have any low-basis stock that I would like to diversify out of? If so, which strategies have I explored to minimize or potentially eliminate the taxes that would be generated?

- What other tax-deferred strategies do I have in place?

---

10   Janet Novak, "Tax-Smart Investing," *Forbes*, June 12, 2000, http://www.forbes.com/forbes/2000/0612/6514280a.html.

In summary, income taxes can create a tremendous drag on investment performance, but controlling tax inefficiencies can increase your total return on investment.

TAX DEFERRAL IN BENEFITS

In chapter 6, we introduced an illustration showing three boxes representing the basic ways that we can defer or avoid paying income taxes when it comes to saving or investing for retirement. We can **deduct** dollars from our earned income, we can **grow** the values from that income on a tax-deferred basis, or we can take an **income** from an account on a tax-free basis. We noted that the IRS will never let us have all three boxes but at most two out of three.

As an employee or business owner, you have the ability to do things now that will help you reduce your taxable income. For example, if you make the maximum contribution to your employer-sponsored retirement plan like a 401(k), a 403(b), or a 457, you will reduce the taxes at the highest point of your personal tax bracket. As a business owner, you may be able to reduce your income by over $50,000 each year depending on your income.

A Personal CFO should work closely with your third party administrator (TPA). A TPA helps manage the creation and record keeping for retirement and benefit plans for businesses. This coordination is important to make sure that you are making the most of your opportunities for reducing income today in your defined contribution plans or determining whether a defined-benefit plan is appropriate. Each discussion with the TPA helps your Personal CFO customize your retirement plan based on the need to maximize your tax planning and growth of your retirement plan. As a business owner, sometimes you may feel like your employees don't appreciate the extra funds that you contribute to their retirement plan. Contributions can come in the form of a discretionary employer match to a 401(k) or 403(b) plan, or a profit-sharing contribution. Your Personal CFO can help your employees understand how fortunate they are to be working for you and having the opportunity to participate in the company retirement plan.

When working with business owners, I like my role as a cheerleader for company morale. Quite often the tax planning is not the only reason you make contributions for your employees. I know this from working with a very successful long-term client who has been generous in making contributions to employees' accounts through both company match and profit sharing. I attended the most recent annual meeting for the retirement plan, and at the conclusion, the business owners and I actually received applause from the employees. It made me feel appreciated, and I'm sure it made the owners of the company very happy that their employees appreciated the additional funds and profit sharing that they have contributed for the benefit of not only their employees but themselves. As an owner of a business, you have the ability to receive benefits yourself, provide your employees a reason to love you, and also receive substantial tax deductions.

STRATEGIES FOR DEDUCTIONS

To get the most benefits from tax strategies, you have to obey the rules. Often that means that waiting until your CPA does your prior year's income taxes will be too late to find out what you could have done. There are some profit-sharing plans that you can implement in the following tax year, but tax-planning strategies generally should be put into action during the tax year in which you are earning the income. When a Personal CFO works with your CPA, they coordinate with him or her on strategies designed to provide the types of deductions that are appropriate for you as a taxpayer. In many cases, tax strategies will provide you with the ability to receive not just deductions but tax credits. These tax credits are harder to find, but if you are incorporated as a business or you're an accredited investor, there may be opportunities for you to invest in things like low-income housing. This investment can provide a tax credit, which is actually a dollar-for-dollar offset of your taxes.

Your Personal CFO also should be making sure you pick deduction strategies that won't be erased by the alternative minimum tax (AMT) calculations that long-form taxpayers have to perform. This involves looking for above-the-line deductions. Like your retirement plan contributions, these are subtracted from your income above the line where you or your accountant enters your adjusted gross income on the IRS Form 1040. So if you are in the 36 percent federal income tax bracket, you would save $0.36 per dollar that you were able to deduct above the line, without any concern for the AMT. The alternative minimum tax is essentially forcing you or your accountant to prepare two different tax returns side by side to determine which one is going to have you pay more. The AMT version can knock out some deductions but not those above the line.

As an example, a unique above-the-line deduction available to investors involves investing in oil and gas partnerships. Of course, a Personal CFO will coordinate and collaborate with their client's CPA to confirm that the investment is appropriate for the client. You should do likewise before considering any such strategy. Like most alternative investments, these programs are available to accredited investors only but provide significant opportunities to receive deductions for high-income earners, or those who had a high-income year because they exercised stock options or sold their company, for example. The investment in energy production provides an up-front tax write-off, subject to some complicated limits. The Personal CFO would review with the client's CPA or tax attorney regarding the amount it can reduce AMT income.

To promote oil and gas exploration, the US government has been allowing deductions from what's called intangible drilling costs since 1913, although the law currently in effect dates to 1986. Originally, this provided an incentive for the industry to drill a lot of exploratory and developmental wells at some risk of failure. Technology has made striking oil much more predictable, but the profitability of any particular program still depends on the price of the fossil fuels. If, for example, it costs $30 a barrel to extract or "lift" the oil out of the ground, and oil happens to be trading at $32 a barrel, then there is limited upside for the investor at that time. The price of oil, like many other commodities, is very volatile in response to many developments worldwide. If oil is trading over $100 a barrel in the prior example, the investor would receive more income from the profits of the well. Investors who are in the highest tax bracket can benefit the most from this tax-planning idea. However, you should also make sure that this decision is made with a plan in mind. As with any investment, there are good programs in oil and gas partnerships, and there are programs that are not as favorable, and new ones are made available every year.

Other tax-planning ideas are very personal and customized to your individual tax situation. For example, there are ways you can benefit from passive losses from past investments. Your Personal CFO would coordinate with your CPA on IRS tax form 8582, which helps your advisors understand if you have any passive losses. If you do, your team can find passive income generators so that you can take advantage of those losses. Matching passive activity losses

(PALs) with a passive income generating (PIG) investment goes by the funny name "PIG/PAL investing."

Most readers are probably already familiar with some more common tax-planning strategies, such as harvesting capital losses to offset capital gains in other investments they sold or wish to sell. A Personal CFO can help them find other strategies like the previous ones.

A Personal CFO will help business owners and professional specialists make sure they are using a tax preparer who has the education and experience necessary to give advice on more complicated strategies. It is important that your CPA understands your comfort level in tax planning. Some CPAs are really aggressive, some are really conservative, and most are appropriately conservative. If a client comes to me to discuss aggressive tax strategies, I draw a horizontal line to represent the relative audit risk for my client. At the left end of the line, I write "no risk." At the opposite end of the line, I write "name a court case after me." That gets people thinking about where they want to be on that line or how far they want to go to save money on taxes.

WHERE ARE YOU ON THE AUDIT RISK SCALE?

NO RISK ←- -→ NAME A COURT CASE AFTER ME

I have found that the best protection is to have a team of advisors who collaborate and coordinate with the others. I had one client whose CPA assisted them in their business but would not collaborate with their attorney or our firm. In the end, the client decided to make a change in order to have a team of advisors able to work together to make good investment, tax, legal, and insurance decisions, as needed. If we're not collaborating and coordinating, there will be gaps and challenges for the client.

The next two chapters extend the horizon for planning even further.

CHAPTER 8

PLANS YOU'LL NEVER SEE THE END OF

When a Personal CFO meets with clients about estate planning, they are interested in how the client defines the word "legacy." How would you like your legacy to be defined by your heirs or your community? Legacy is defined as a bequest of money or property or anything handed down from one generation to another. How prepared are you to leave the legacy that you want to leave for your family and community? Is that financial legacy going to go fully to those whom you want to receive it?

Years ago, I had a retired client who lived in the small town of West Point City, Utah. He was an old farmer who was completely committed to his family, his faith, and his community. He would call me from time to time to ask me, as his advisor, if he still had enough money to buy an ice cream cone. I would always laugh and assure him that he had enough to buy not only himself an ice cream cone but also every member of his large, extended family, as well as every family in the little town of West Point City.

I think he just liked to know that he was doing just fine. Loy Blake passed away in 2002 when he was in his early nineties but not before he was able to leave quite a legacy to his family, faith, and community. In fact, his family still likes to go out on the anniversary of his death and have ice cream in honor of "Grandpa Blake." Although Loy had several occupations, he considered himself a farmer. He loved the farmland and the people of West Point City, which he called "God's country." He was the first mayor of West Point City and held that position for over twenty years. Back when

Loy Blake

there were few if any municipal services, he would even drive the city snowplow to clear the roads after a snowstorm. Now that's dedication, from someone who loved the city and the people who lived there.

Loy's favorite project while mayor was the development of West Point Park. This thirty-acre park became a community gathering place. After his death, the city renamed the park Loy F. Blake Park.

Loy was a valiant servant of his church. He served as bishop of the West Point congregation of The Church of Jesus Christ of Latter-day Saints for ten years, among many other church assignments. He and his wife, Erma, completed two missions for the church as well.

Loy made a new friend wherever he went. Driving through town, he honked and waved at everyone. His greatest joy was being surrounded by his family. He had a special relationship with every child and grandchild, reminding each to "remember who you are." Loy was a man of service, wisdom, warmth, and generosity, and his family continues to carry on his legacy today, thanks in part to many different estate-planning strategies put in place for the Blake family over the years.

I know that Loy and Erma would be thrilled with the legacy that continues to be carried on. Assisting the Blake family in coordination with their other advisors has been rewarding personally and professionally. With the planning that has been done, the family has been able to receive income and assets to assist them with their desires to serve their family, their faith, and their communities. Because of his example, his legacy lives on through his children, grandchildren, and great-grandchildren, who are involved in serving within their communities and church. For example, his daughter Susan and son-in-law Gordon Carter established a charitable organization, Charity Anywhere Foundation, which has been involved in service projects all over the world since the 1990s. Their foundation motto is "Be Good, Do Good". I am sure that Erma and Loy Blake are pleased as they look down from heaven on the legacy they left.

A CONTINUING PROCESS

Some people believe that once you complete your will or a trust, you are done and have no need to continue to plan or adjust your plans. Maybe they never heard this joke: "What's the difference between death and taxes? Death doesn't get any worse when Congress goes into session." Funny, and like a lot of jokes it contains some truth. In fact, there have been multiple changes to the estate tax law over our lifetimes.

In 2016, we "celebrate" the hundred-year anniversary of the inception of the federal estate tax, but it has been around much longer than that. According to the book *Inheritance and Wealth in America* (Plenum Press, 1998):

Taxation of property transfers at death can be traced back to ancient Egypt as early as 700 BC. Nearly 2,000 years ago, Roman emperor Caesar Augustus imposed the *Vicesina Hereditatium*, a tax on successions and legacies to all but close relatives. Taxes imposed at the death of a family member were quite common in feudal Europe, often amounting to a family's annual property rent. By the eighteenth century, stamp duties and registration fees on wills, inventories, and other documents related to property transfers at death had been adopted by many nations, including that of the newly formed United States of America.

How does this affect you? Laws at the state and federal level seek to limit the financial legacy that you have worked so hard to build, and the government continues to find more ways to become one of your beneficiaries. Your estate can really go in one of three directions. To illustrate this, suppose for a moment that the estate tax were voluntary. What percentage of your assets would you like to allocate to each of the following?

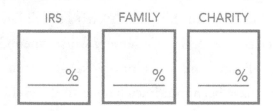

In the mid-1990s I was hired by a small-business owner in Northern California whose estate value was in excess of $20 million. Several years later, I asked him and his wife this exact question: "What percentage of your assets would you like to allocate to the IRS, your family, or charity?" Sorry, IRS, but they did not want to give you anything.

They wanted their financial legacy to be allocated to their children and to the charities they had grown to love and support throughout their lives. I remember asking them if they wanted us to help them build a zero estate tax plan. Their response was, "Can you do that?" I assured them that in my opinion, federal estate taxes were voluntary, especially if the couple was philanthropic, which in this case they were.

So, in collaboration with their long-time CPA and one of my associates in The Resource Group, we introduced them to new legal counsel and set off to create this "zero estate tax plan." The creativity spawned by the collaboration of this team of professionals was so great we were asked to educate other advisors throughout the nation who were part of the Sagemark Consulting Private Wealth Services group.

WHAT IS THE RESOURCE GROUP?

Lincoln Financial Network, the retail wealth management affiliate of Lincoln Financial Group (NYSE:LNC), operates an invitation-only, nationwide network of the top two hundred planners affiliated with its Lincoln Financial Advisors. The goal of The Resource Group is to collaborate, share intellectual capital—including financial-planning expertise, resources, networking opportunities, and practice management strategies—and partner with home office executives and committee concierge support to help drive practice development among advisors and provide industry-leading service to clients.

David Stone was elected as chairman of the board of The Resource Group in 2015.

IS THE IRS ONE OF YOUR BENEFICIARIES?

A common problem over the years in estate planning has to do with ownership and beneficiary designations in life insurance. Let's assume that you have about $1 million of life insurance, payable at death to your spouse or business. Based on the size of your estate, your current life insurance ownership and beneficiary structure may inadvertently make the IRS the beneficiary of up to half of your insurance proceeds. I'm sure that's not what you had in mind.

Most people are surprised by this because they believe that life insurance is tax-free. In fact, it is income tax-free, but unless you plan, it is generally estate taxable. Were you aware of this? My guess is probably not. Let me show you what I mean.

To the extent that you, your spouse, or your business own the $1 million of insurance on your life and it is payable to your spouse or business, it will be taxed in the survivor's estate. As a result, your family will pay unnecessary estate taxes on the insurance proceeds. If you are in the 40 percent marginal estate-tax bracket, the IRS would be the beneficiary of $400,000 of your $1 million of life insurance! That's a lot of unnecessary taxes, isn't it?

But the problem is actually worse than that. What your children lose, they lose for their entire lifetimes. Under the Rule of 72, a general principle that helps explain how money grows through compounding, assets growing at 7 percent double in value every ten years. So the $400,000 actually costs your children $800,000 if they outlive you and your spouse by ten years, $1.6 million if they outlive you by twenty years, and $3.2 million if they outlive you by thirty years, and the impact just gets worse over time.

Most of my clients would be concerned about that, but that doesn't mean it's important to you. Is structuring your life insurance to not only be income tax-free but also estate tax-free important to you? Well, that's certainly something a Personal CFO can help you accomplish.

For example, I had a client in Southern California with a sizable estate who needed to create a death benefit for his wife. Before he came to Stone Consulting Group for advice, he had taken his company pension as a life-only benefit. In other words, if he died first, she would no longer have his pension and would be reliant on Social Security and any other assets that they had. We collaborated with their attorney to create a spousal lifetime access trust (or SLAT) that would be the owner and beneficiary of the life insurance policy on the husband, rather than it being part of his estate.

In this case, the husband lived a few more years, until 2012. When the death benefit was paid, the assets were not included in the estate, and no estate or income taxes were due. In addition, the children of the client will be able to have the assets without having to pay the IRS for access to the funds. We were able to remove the IRS as a beneficiary of my client's estate. Smart planning paid off for this client, who was the son of Loy Blake in West Point City, Utah. Interesting how the legacy of Loy Blake lives on.

Most people are not aware of the amount of estate taxes that could be owed. What planning strategies have you employed to reduce taxes? What if some of your assets could be moved outside your estate to avoid paying estate taxes on them? Would that make sense for you in your situation? For many business owners, these taxes could end up being financially devastating to their legacy or vision of that legacy, and we come back to that in chapter 10.

Wouldn't you prefer to have your loved ones receive the maximum amount possible and not be burdened with liquidating assets to pay taxes? The Personal CFO will help to calculate your estate taxes today and into the future. More importantly, the CFO will educate you on all the relevant strategies designed to reduce estate taxes and in some cases avoid them altogether. Is this something worth exploring? It has been rewarding to help my clients visualize their legacy and make it a reality through the Power of a Plan.

CHAPTER 9

GENERATIONAL WEALTH PLANNING

In 2007, I saw a movie called *The Ultimate Gift*. The story is about a young man named Jason Stevens who lives a life of wealth and privilege. When his grandfather, played by James Garner, dies, Jason expects to receive a large inheritance. Instead, however, through pre-recorded video messages from his grandfather, Jason must pass tests along a journey of life lessons to discover and earn the true gift his grandfather meant for him to receive.

The story portrayed how Jason's extended family relationships had been negatively affected by wealth. Along the way, Jason befriended a dying girl and her mother and learned what was really important in life. After viewing this movie, I decided that it would be a nice gift for a select group of our high-net-worth clients. The overall message of the movie highlighted the importance of family relationships and the great personal satisfaction that comes from thinking of others and not getting caught up in self-aggrandizement.

A wealthy client once said, "I want my children's inheritance to bless their lives and the lives of their children and grandchildren, not curse their lives." He had seen others who had made decisions regarding their wealth without preparing their heirs to be good stewards of that wealth. Preparing the next generation to receive wealth can be as important as the strategies used for estate planning. However, determining how your assets will be distributed is just the first step.

Generational wealth planning aims to prepare your heirs to receive the wealth that you have spent a lifetime creating, growing, preserving, and protecting. A client study from Wilmington Trust Corp. completed in 2011 showed that 90 percent of the wealth of those surveyed could be gone by the end of the third generation. That means that 90 percent of your wealth could be gone by the end of your grandchildren's lives.

So what happens to your great-grandchildren? What happens to your family legacy? Like any responsible parent, you want your children and grandchildren to learn the importance of personal initiative, hard work, and social responsibility. Are you concerned that inheriting money may become a disincentive to their self-motivation, productivity, and achievement? You are not alone.

You may personally know wealthy families whose descendants inherit significant wealth and become unmotivated, unproductive spendthrifts who eventually squander their inheritance. The phenomenon, sometimes called "shirt sleeves to shirt sleeves in three generations," is the lesson in *The Ultimate Gift*. You can take some simple steps to ensure that this doesn't happen to your family, your vision, or your wealth.[11]

FAMILY MISSION AND PHILOSOPHY

The process starts with engaging your children and other family members in an open, meaningful conversation, one that is not about money but rather focuses on your family's mission and philosophy.

11   Generational Wealth Planning brochure, Lincoln Financial Advisors 10/14.

After all, your valuables are only part of your legacy. Passing down your values will help ensure that future generations understand and appreciate that while money brings advantages, it is tempered with the obligations and responsibilities that you instill in your descendants.[12]

My younger brother, Stephen, recently celebrated his fiftieth birthday. There's a tradition in the Stone family that we go around the room and say one nice thing about the person celebrating his or her birthday. When it came to my turn, I thought of the Scout Law from the Boy Scouts of America. My older brother, Ron, said, "No fair. That's what I was going to say." So we shared the Scout Law together that we believed was a representation of not only our brother's life but our father's as well.

Four Eagle Scouts from the Stone family
(Front: David & his father Ronald V. "Bud", back: Stephen and Ron).

A Scout is trustworthy, loyal, helpful, friendly, courteous, kind, obedient, cheerful, thrifty, brave, clean, and reverent. You see, my dad and his three brothers were all Eagle Scouts, which was an unusual thing back in the 1940s when he received his Eagle. Since the

---

12 Quote from Generational Wealth Planning brochure, Lincoln Financial Advisors 10/14 CRN-1039575-101714.

inception of the Eagle Scout award in 1912, 2.01 percent of eligible Scouts have earned Scouting's highest honor. In 2014, 6.01 percent of eligible Scouts earned the Eagle Scout award.[13] Even though the percentage has increased over the years, it is still a very small percentage of young men in scouting who receive this honor. The Eagle tradition in the Stone family continued with my two brothers and me also receiving our Eagle awards and almost all of our cousins as well.

I have two sons. My older son, Chandler, is an Eagle Scout, and my younger son, Colton, is close to being an Eagle Scout as well. These values have been instilled in our family for generations. Often there are unique family traits and qualities or characteristics that define your family or your legacy.

Best-selling author Stephen R. Covey is well known for the book *The 7 Habits of Highly Effective People*. A lesser-known sequel was a book he wrote in the late 1990s, *The 7 Habits of Highly Effective Families*. In his blog a decade later, Covey wrote about a presentation on strengthening families in crisis in 2009. Many audience members had lost their jobs and found themselves looking for work in a tough situations that easily caused neglect, fear, and withdrawal—a true snapshot of the nation at the time:

> In such situations, I counsel people to remember who are the most important people in their lives and what matters most to them. Yes, being out of a job might have you in a crisis, but your family is your most precious possession. So what can you do to strengthen your family in times of trouble?

---

13   "What percentage of Boy Scouts become Eagle Scouts?" Bryan Wendall, Bryan on Scouting, last modified March 30, 2015, http://blog.scoutingmag azine.org/2015/03/30/what-percentage-of-boy-scouts-become-eagle-scouts/.

There are three things that I encourage everyone to do with their families in good times or bad:

1. **Write a family mission statement**. Identify what kind of family you want to be. For instance, what qualities define your family, what kinds of feelings do you want in your home, how do you want to build relationships? Get everyone involved in these questions and write something that describes your family and how you want to be.

2. **Hold weekly family meetings**. Gather your family once a week to talk about issues, problems, or good things in your family. Refer to your mission statement to see how you are doing. Enjoy this time together; do something fun.

3. **Remember the emotional bank account**. Similar to a bank account, you can make deposits or withdrawals from each of your family relationships. Make a conscious effort to make meaningful deposits in your relationships. When you make a withdrawal, apologize and correct the mistake.

Strengthening your relationships strengthens your family. Taking control over your life rather than weathering problems will make you more effective in job searches, and your family will be your greatest source of strength and support.

GENERATIONAL WEALTH PLANNING STARTS AT HOME

Having an effective generational wealth plan takes effort, but it is worth it. Many questions come to mind that you might ask yourself. When do you start generational wealth planning? The answer is the sooner the better. It's important to have a broad education, but you should especially devote sufficient time to education on financial topics. This would include parents and grandparents relating their personal experiences. These stories can make a significant impact on your children and grandchildren.

While trying to teach my own children to be good stewards of their financial resources, I dreamed up an idea called the Daddy 401(k). I told my son Chandler and daughter Katelyn at a very young age, "If you save your own money, Daddy will match it dollar for dollar in the Daddy 401(k) plan." I remember walking by my son's room—he was the first to take me up on the offer—and hearing the seven-year-old tell his nine-year-old sister, "I made $25 last month, and I didn't have to do anything."

Katelyn's response was an enthusiastic "Nuh-uh." Chandler had doubled his birthday gift money. She said, "How did you do that?" Chandler's response was, "I put $25 in the Daddy 401(k) plan and Daddy invested for me and I saw it went up to $50. You can do it too if you put money in the Daddy 401(k) plan," and she did. Both of them have made contributions, as have their siblings, and have participated in the benefit of the Daddy 401(k) plan because I actually invested the money in a mutual fund, and it did go up.

What I told my kids is that when they earned money or received money as gifts, they would split it up into three pieces. They would take the first 10 percent and give it to charity. Next, they would take half of the full amount and put that into the "Daddy 401(k) plan" to save for long-term things like college, a car, or something they would want later in life. All my kids have their money set aside for things like education or, in my son's case, a wedding ring one day in the future.

If they got $100, they could spend $40 on anything they wanted right away, even candy. I didn't restrict that 40 percent at all, but I found that they were less likely to spend it than save it for something big that they wanted later. My older kids are still really good savers. Chandler has graduated from college and is investing every month. Katelyn and her husband, Marcus, who is in medical school, are also great savers and are committed to making good financial decisions. They all tell me that the education they received as children helped them see the benefit of building a nest egg for the future as adults.

ONE COUPLE'S STORY

Another question in generational wealth planning is who should be involved, the answer to which is unique to every family. However, when you and your spouse can be present, the impact of those family values and their ongoing legacy becomes more realized. I saw this take place within one of my client's families.

I was introduced to Mary and Robert by their son, Ralph, who was a client of mine. Mary and Robert were in their eighties and were interviewing me to determine whether or not they wanted to hire our firm to assist them with their comprehensive financial planning. At the time, Robert was a financial "do-it-yourselfer." He enjoyed becoming knowledgeable about investing and insurance, and, being retired, had plenty of time to be involved in this. And he also fancied himself as being somewhat organized.

Within a year of our meeting, I received a phone call from Robert's son, Ralph. He informed me that his father had passed away unexpectedly and that the family needed help to organize their financial affairs and take care of his mother. I went to Mary's home in the San Francisco Bay Area, rolled up my sleeves, and began to look through the family's filing cabinet to help put her financial house in order. We found that Robert had done a good job of organizing his financial records. This was helpful for me as a Personal CFO.

After hearing Mary talk about her children and grandchildren, we determined that she had a passion to help them become educated in financial matters because "that is what Robert would have wanted." We decided to create what we called "the Grandma 401(k) plan." As you might have guessed, this was a variation on the Daddy 401(k) plan that I explained previously. Robert had done a good job of setting money aside for his grandchildren and children in trust accounts, as well as custodial accounts that we could use to benefit them.

I had the opportunity to work closely with not only Mary and Robert's children but also their grandchildren on the benefits of investing for the long term. All of the grandchildren are no longer minors, so their accounts are in their own names as they continue to save and invest. Educating the grandchildren has brought them great advantage in preparing to receive their future inheritance.

In estate planning, you work tirelessly to provide benefits to those you love. Generational wealth planning provides you a way to prepare your family to receive that wealth and to be good stewards of that wealth. Having the opportunity to educate and inspire the grandchildren of Robert and Mary has made an impact on me as an advisor and served as a reminder of why we do the things we do for our children and grandchildren.

I remember one time when I was meeting with Mary's son, her daughter-in-law, and her twenty-year-old grandson. The discussion was focused on being compassionate and giving. These were very important values to Mary and Robert. I had introduced a YouTube video that we viewed to illustrate this point. The four of us—a physician, an architect, a college student, and their advisor—shared an emotional moment together that helped strengthen their grandson's commitment to the personal and financial values of Mary and

Robert. Even in this situation, it was not too late to start and to assist them with their generational wealth planning.

QUESTIONS TO ASK YOURSELF

To help get you started determining how you want to have your wealth pass on to the next generation, ask yourself these questions:

- What comes to mind when you think about your financial wealth and your children?

- What types of conversations do you and your children have about money and wealth?

- What worries you about the future of your children?

- What two or three things have helped you achieve your level of success?

- Is it important to you that your heirs know you and what you stood for?

- What are the two or three things you'd hope your grandchildren would say about you? What does it mean to you to be a member of the (your name) family?

- What do you want to be sure your children and grandchildren have in life?

Proactive generational wealth planning will help future generations appreciate what it took you to build and maintain your wealth, embrace your values and beliefs, and ultimately become outstanding stewards of those values and beliefs and not just your money.[14]

14 Quote from Generational Wealth Planning brochure, Lincoln Financial Advisors.

The next chapter focuses on business owner planning. It's followed by a conclusion, wrapping up all the major points of this book.

CHAPTER 10

LET'S TALK BUSINESS

Business owners are busy people. Successful business owners are even busier. Those individuals need someone to help them, just as when you want to lose weight you find a workout partner to make sure you go to the gym. If you don't have someone holding you accountable, it makes it challenging to be successful with your business and financial goals. That's part of the role of the Personal CFO—just helping people be organized and get their financial house in order.

When I first met Dr. Carl Smith, he had a negative net worth. I introduced to him the Financial-Planning Wheel of Fortune and the benefits of having a Personal CFO. He jumped all over it, because he's a successful dentist and very busy. He has over two dozen associates and staff in his practice, is active in his church and community, and has a large family.

In one of our first meetings, Carl told me he knew there were things he should be doing, but he just didn't have time. He decided to hire our firm. In the process, I worked with him and his wife on their personal financial planning first, and then we began to work toward dealing with his business owner planning. He's an excellent dentist, but he needed some direction and some coaching as it related to the financial aspects of his business.

We began their business owner planning by working on their employee benefits, helping them put together a 401(k) plan, profit-sharing plan, health plan, and life insurance. We had an employee meeting to educate the employees and coordinate with their office manager on how the enrollment and record keeping should be done. We brought in a third-party administrator who helped us design a retirement plan that included employer contributions. This kind of benefit helps employees feel valued and helps the employer retain key, long-term employees.

Next we tried to work with Carl's accountant, but unfortunately he was unresponsive about returning my calls—or Carl's. We offered referrals to a number of accountants, and Carl chose a new accountant. Then we coordinated with that accountant and persuaded Carl of the need and importance of hiring a bookkeeper. Carl now has a bookkeeper who is also a CPA helping him keep on top of his business's financial statements. This provides us with more data so that we can help Carl stay organized and reach his long-term goals. During the time that we have worked with him, he went from paying rent to purchasing his office building. He has refinanced it, is doing a home remodel, and is saving and investing on a monthly basis. I'm happy to report that his net worth has increased substantially over the time we've been working with him. In about five years, he went from a negative net worth to being a multimillionaire.

Now that his financial affairs are organized to minimize debt and maximize his resources, Carl can place more energy into being a dentist instead of having to deal with all the business issues that arise for a business owner.

Business owners should decide where to focus their energy. There are only so many days in a week and hours in a day. You may want to focus on growing company sales or creating an exceptional workplace environment for your key employees. You should also consider strategic business owner planning issues because they will inevitably arise and affect not only your customers, clients, or patients but also your key employees and associates. In addition, in some cases your business decisions can also affect your family. Whether you are creating, buying, or selling a business or dealing with a succession or continuity crisis or some other issue, having a team of professionals working together in collaboration can be the difference between leaving behind a legacy of success or a nightmare for your heirs.

On more than one occasion, I have been approached by clients to help them establish new business ventures. These were exceptional professionals who had successful practices but needed business plans. Not all professionally licensed specialists have a desire to be business owners. Some prefer to stay affiliated with a law or accounting firm, medical group, or dental company, but many of you would prefer to grow your own business, creating future wealth for you and your family.

A Personal CFO typically likes working with business owners because the two have much in common. Most business owners have a desire to take their plans to the next level. This is usually due to their hope to grow their businesses for the benefit of their clients, their employees, and their families. For most of my business owner clients, their business is their most valuable asset. And our conversations about business owner planning help make it more successful.

Some of the questions a Personal CFO would ask you include:

- How is your business structured? Are you operating as a sole proprietorship, C corporation, S corporation, partnership, or LLC? (These types are explained under Business Structures on the next page.)

- Are you the majority owner? Would that be 51 percent, 100 percent, or somewhere in between?

- Is the stock or partnership LLC interest titled in your name? Is the other percentage of stock or beneficial interest owned by someone in your family?

- Do you have any other family members other than those who own stock involved in the business with you? If yes, who are they? What is their relationship to you? How old are they? How long have they been in the business?

- Do you have other children who are not involved in the business? If so, how many kids do you have and what are their ages?[15]

As you can see, there is an overlap between business owner planning and estate planning in discussing family dynamics with your advisor.

BUSINESS STRUCTURES

There are several different types of business structures. These definitions come from the federal Small Business Administration, which explains more about the advantages and limitations of each structure on its website:

- A sole proprietorship is the most basic type of business to establish. You alone own the company and are responsible for its assets and liabilities.

- There are several different types of partnerships, which depend on the nature of the arrangement and partner responsibility for the business.

---

15 Lincoln Financial Advisors Business Planning.

- An LLC, or limited liability company, is designed to provide the limited liability features of a corporation and the tax efficiencies and operational flexibility of a partnership.

- People form cooperatives to meet a collective need or to provide a service that benefits all member-owners.

- A corporation (sometimes referred to as a C corporation) is an independent legal entity owned by shareholders. This means that the corporation, not the shareholders that own it, is held legally liable for the actions and debts the business incurs.

- An eligible domestic corporation can avoid double taxation (once to the corporation and again to the shareholders) by electing to be treated by the IRS as an S corporation. Shareholders are taxed only on the personal level.

CONTINUITY AND SUCCESSION

If something happened to you tomorrow, what would happen to your business? Do you have a contingency plan if something unexpected happens to you so that your business can continue to run? Do you have a purchase and sales agreement, commonly called a buy-sell agreement, that spells out the disposition of your business interest in the event of what Lincoln Financial Advisors calls "the eight Ds" of business succession planning? All eight Ds are explained in the following pages, but first let's define the buy-sell agreement. It is a document that specifically delineates the terms and conditions agreed to by the parties in case a partner leaves the business. It is not a plan but a contractual document that is the end product of the planning process and is a reflection of the understanding the parties have reached through the planning process. An effective agreement addresses the rights and obligations of the parties in the event of any of these eight Ds:

1. Death. The purchase of shares either by the corporation or other individuals is obviously mandatory.

2. Disability. Disability and permanent disability should be defined. Valuation and terms of payment should be defined. Will salary continuation payments during a disability period be deducted from the purchase price? Will disability insurance be purchased?

3. Departure, such as shareholder's retirement or decision to pursue other opportunities or interests. All the possibilities for voluntary departure should be addressed, along with what happens to the ownership share: transfer to family members, first rights of refusal, and so on.

4. Divorce. Provisions should be included to protect shareholders from hostile spousal separation situations. All spouses must be required to sign the buy-sell agreement.

5. Deadlock. Provisions should be included to resolve disagreements by equal owners and provide for liquidation if normal operations cannot be resumed.

6. Disagreement. Provisions should be included to resolve disagreements resulting in minority owners being forced out of the business and purchasing their interests.

7. Default. Because individual shareholders generally must personally guarantee business loans, an individual shareholder's default or bankruptcy may also need to trigger a mandatory buyout of his or her interests.

8. Determination of value. Each shareholder wants to have a fair value for his or her interest. This must be established initially and should include provisions and methodologies to update it periodically.[16]

Some of these eight Ds are not easy to talk about. Quite often, individuals will not actually believe that they're so disabled they can't work, even though they haven't been in the office for six months. By having a discussion in the planning process about disability, you can identify what criteria would be used to determine if a person is disabled. As for divorce, some clients don't even want to discuss it as a possibility. They feel that their marriage is so solid that they'll never have to worry about it. I wish that were always the case, but unfortunately over half of all marriages end in divorce. After some discussion, I find that most clients can understand the issues that might be faced by the spouse of an owner who dies or a co-owner who would have to begin dealing with the deceased business partner's spouse. Even though it is difficult to work through these types of issues as part of a buy-sell agreement, it should be done.

Assuming you have a buy-sell agreement, what value does it place on your business? Do you still agree with that value? If you do not have a buy-sell agreement, what would you estimate the value of your business is today? If you're struggling with that question, maybe I can ask you in a different way.

---

16 Lincoln Financial Advisors: National Planning Department.

If I were to write you a check today for your business, how much would you sell it for? If I owned your business, how much would you be willing to write me a check for? If you can answer those two questions, the Personal CFO might take those two numbers, split the difference, and consider that a ballpark value for your business in today's dollars. How do you feel about that?

In many cases, business owners do not have a buy-sell agreement. Five things can happen as a result:

- In the event of your death, you haven't created a market for your stock, both as to price and buyer.

- In the event of a business partner's death, you haven't created an agreement regarding his or her spouse and/or children.

- In the event of a divorce, your spouse or your partner's spouse may get 50 percent of the stock.

- In the event of personal bankruptcy, either your creditors or your partner's creditors may get the ownership of your business.

- If you or your business partner becomes disabled and cannot make a material contribution to the day-to-day operations of the business, you don't have a plan for how the company will function in his or her absence.

If you do have a buy-sell agreement in place, your Personal CFO should consider whether the type of plan you have is appropriate for you and for your business partners or shareholders. Common types of buy-sell agreements include a stock redemption, cross-purchase, or "Wait and See." We'll discuss each of those, but first let's look at how a buy-sell agreement can be funded or unfunded.

If a buy-sell agreement were unfunded, your partner would have to come up with a way to pay to purchase the stock or beneficial interest in the business from you or your surviving spouse if the need arose. They might be required to borrow money to buy out your deceased partner's spouse. In a funded plan, you purchase a life insurance policy on your business partner to pay for a purchase or a portion of a purchase resulting from death. You can also acquire a buy-sell policy that covers disability. In that case, an independent third party would be making the decision of whether or not your disability qualifies under the terms of your buy-sell agreement. This is important because at some point, you may or may not agree on whether or not you are disabled or your business partner is disabled.

Many factors go into determining which type of buy-sell agreement would be most effective for you as a business owner. Of course, there are pros and cons to all the options. A stock redemption plan is one of the most common buy-sell agreements if there are multiple owners involved. However, if it provides for the corporation to buy back a deceased stockholder's interest in the business, taxes may be a concern. The problem is that under current tax law, your agreement will trigger excessive capital gains tax consequences when the survivor sells his business interest. Let me give you an example.

Assume your corporation is worth $10 million, $5 million is yours, and $5 million is your business partner's. You started, like most entrepreneurs, on a tiny budget, meaning your original cost basis is close to zero. Your partner dies, and the corporation redeems his stock using life insurance proceeds. You now own 100 percent of the corporation worth $10 million with your original cost basis of zero. When you sell the business, you'll be paying capital gains taxes on $10 million. At a tax rate of 20 percent, you would owe $2 million. And that doesn't even take into account state income taxes as applicable.

By restructuring your current buy-sell agreement, you can reduce the capital gains tax by 50 percent, saving you $1 million in the previous example. Of course, there are times when the stock redemption buy-sell agreement is a more appropriate option, but typically that would be when there are a large number of owners, making the use of a cross-purchase agreement difficult or expensive to fund and administer.

Depending on the type of buy-sell agreement you have, it's possible that the surviving stockholders will be required to buy the deceased stockholder's business interest. A cross-purchase agreement potentially becomes a problem if there is no flexibility to adjust the timing of the stock purchase to corporate and personal financial conditions. In designing a buy-sell agreement today, we don't know what the federal income tax and estate tax law will be when the business is sold. We don't know whether you'll be operating as a C corporation or an S corporation, and we don't know the impact of alternative minimum tax on your transaction. We don't know whether the surviving stockholder will want to keep or sell the business and how that will affect your cost basis. We don't know what the corporate and personal financial positions will be in the company and whether or not you will be able to fund the purchase or sale at the time of the transaction.[17]

Each of these factors will determine the optimum method of the stock purchase. The best time to make this decision is not today if mandated under some agreements but rather at the death of a stockholder. If you have a "wait and see" buy-sell agreement, this will usually provide you with more flexibility and perhaps be the best

17   Lincoln Financial Advisors Business Planning.

solution for your business partners. Like other major decisions in your planning, it is important for your Personal CFO, attorney, and CPA to collaborate on this decision (see Appendix E).

BUSINESS STRUCTURE

Earlier in the chapter, I discussed choosing the right entity for your business. If you were operating under a C corporation, as opposed to a subchapter S corporation, in light of current tax law, your Personal CFO along with your CPA should evaluate whether electing an S status might be more advantageous for you for these reasons:

- The S corporation provides a single tax on corporate income as opposed to two taxes, one to the corporation and one to the shareholder.

- Electing S status avoids the double tax on liquidation or disposition of appreciated assets out of the current C corporation.

- S status eliminates the current alternative minimum tax.

These are just a few of the types of questions that a Personal CFO would want to discuss with regard to which entity you use for your business. Of course, your Personal CFO, CPA, and attorney should collaborate to develop a business plan that would be in your best interest and the best interest of the company.

A common question asked by business owners is, "How much should I take in salary versus take in draw or corporate profit?" That recommendation is important to make in collaboration with the CPA. You should also consider the current Social Security wage limit. Balancing how much income you want through company payroll to maximize profit-sharing contributions or match to a 401(k) plan should also be taken into consideration. Whether you have an S or a

C corporation will make a difference because that changes how you're taxed specifically as it relates to Social Security and Medicare taxes. Whether you're an LLC, a partnership, or a sole proprietor will also affect that decision.

Sometimes in business owner planning, an owner will decide to change structure from a C corporation to an S corporation. There are a lot of different elements that need to be coordinated and decisions that should be made. If your goal is to maximize your retirement plan contributions, then your Personal CFO may recommend you run money through a C corporation differently than through an S or an LLC. A lot of times people don't think about tax strategies until it's too late. That's why you should plan ahead.

I had a phone call with a new client and his CPA in which we were comparing what he expected to owe in taxes in 2015 compared to what he paid in taxes in 2014. One of the recommendations involved maximizing the client's deductions in 2015 by contributing a larger amount into the company 401(k) plan before the end of the year. Unfortunately, the client wasn't actively receiving communications from the broker running his 401(k) plan. We contacted the plan's third-party administrator (TPA) and uncovered how low employee participation in the plan was limiting his allowable contributions. This information was helpful to better understand the issues behind his limitations. The client could change the plan to triple his own contribution limits and maximize his tax deduction. Unfortunately, the TPA informed us that the client had missed the deadline by three days to notify the employees of the change. That meant he couldn't make the change in 2016. Moving forward with a Personal CFO coordinating the effort, the client's advisory team will be more proactive while keeping track of such deadlines to make appropriate decisions.

BUSINESS VALUATION

There are attorneys, CPAs, and entire companies that specialize in doing business valuations. The cost of the service can run anywhere from $500 to $50,000 or more, depending on what you need and how big your organization is. The valuation can be very helpful in deciding whether to sell or buy a business. Then there are some business owners and prospective purchasers who will simply write a number for the price they want to get or pay, seal it up in an envelope, and give it to a third party to see if there can be a deal. That may happen if somebody really wants to get out when a partnership is not working, and they say, "Look, I need to either buy you out or you need to buy me out." They each write down the price at which they would be willing to buy or sell.

Business valuation also comes up in the case of an owner who simply wants to move on to other opportunities. In that situation, your Personal CFO can help coordinate with the owner's legal counsel to set up an installment sale or "earn out."

WHAT IF YOU'RE REALLY SUCCESSFUL?

What if you've grown your company to the point where you're looking to sell to an outside entity? If your company has a value of $10 million or more, you might be a candidate for specialists who work to deliver mergers and acquisitions services. These specialists fill a need for the small- to middle-market business that is looking to sell and has a value between $10 million and $500 million. On the stock exchanges, a company between $100 million and $1 billion in market capitalization is considered a small-cap or a mini- cap stock.

Through our strategic business partners at Lincoln Financial Advisors, I have dealt with many organizations, from manufacturing companies to retail stores, to help them identify opportunities to sell their companies. These strategic partners have done many transactions where they have collaborated with investment banks throughout the United States. If your business qualifies for this type of work, your Personal CFO should assist you and your existing team to close the biggest transaction of your life. These buyers can be strategic buyers who are in similar industries or buyers who are not currently in your industry. Private equity firms are potential buyers. They will look at the success you've had and determine whether their stockholders will profit by providing additional capital and growing opportunities in your industry, the ultimate goal typically being to grow your company and then flip it to turn a profit.

Years ago, I was working closely with a convenience store chain that's mostly in the Midwest. My associates and I were involved in creating a marketability assessment for sale of the business. The owner was using an attorney who did not have experience in this type of transaction. When we introduced the investment banking firm that we thought would be the best fit for this transaction, the company owner decided to stay with his local attorney. He just thought that our mergers and acquisitions legal specialist would be too expensive. But after the whole saga played out, his attorney had charged him several hundred thousand dollars more—double the fees the investment bank firm quoted for the transaction. We think that it's important to work with specialists who have experience and are not learning on your dollar. Because that's what the convenience store owner's attorney was doing.

In contrast, our business specialist strategic partners were able to use an investment banking firm that we've worked with to help a health-care company client complete a sale of the business. The price, nearly $50 million, was nearly double what the client originally hoped for. A professionally done marketability assessment helps you better understand the viability of a sale. These types of transactions are usually for small- to medium-size companies that are not large enough to list on any stock exchange but are larger than a typical transaction that would involve a simple buy-sell agreement.

LEGACY ISSUES

There are many other issues around business owner planning that should be addressed for business owners. Let's see if some of these apply to you. You may not even have decided whether you're going to keep or sell the business upon your retirement. In addition, you may have children who are working in your business. If you have a son or daughter active in the business, you may need a mechanism to transfer the ownership to that son or daughter and then take the balance of your estate and pass it on to your other children.

Let's suppose that the total value of your estate can be equally divided with your sons or daughters who are active in the business and receive the business. One question would be whether you have taken into account the impact of estate taxes, which will be levied against your total estate. What happens if the amount your other children are due comes up considerably short because the nonbusiness assets had to be liquidated to pay the IRS? In some cases, businesses have had to be sold to pay estate taxes. So in business owner planning and estate planning, it's very important to coordinate these efforts and make sure you provide ways to create liquidity for the payment of those taxes. A forced sale of the assets may be necessary and possibly even the sale of your entire business.

My question to you would be, "Does this concern you?" Would it be worth explaining ways to transfer your business that would maximize your ability to equalize your estate among your children and minimize the impact of estate taxes? The Personal CFO can help.

EMPLOYEE BENEFITS

The last area of business owner planning that we'll discuss is your employee benefit plans for you and your associates. The most common one is the company retirement plan. It is important when establishing a company retirement plan that your Personal CFO collaborate not only with your CPA but also with a TPA to help you optimize benefits for you and your employees. It is also important through this collaboration that your Personal CFO help with and stay on top of communication with the employees. A common mistake made by business owners is failure to recognize that they are the trustees of their retirement plan and have a fiduciary responsibility to educate their employees about how they, as plan participants, are to invest their money in their company retirement plan.

There are ways that the business owner can pass on fiduciary responsibility to professional money managers who will handle the education and communications with employees. Recently I had a meeting with one of my clients' workforce. In this annual meeting, we discussed the importance and significance of having what is called a qualified default investment alternative (QDIA). We educated the employees, as we do each year, about the many options that they have for their retirement money and why the owners of the business determined that the QDIA would provide them investment management expertise.

My making this type of presentation is not just about reducing or removing the fiduciary responsibility that the owners would have as the trustee. It is also about helping their employees better understand the great benefit of working for my clients' companies. My goal is to help improve and increase company morale while providing the employees information and education on their current retirement plan.

A newer issue involves the changing role of employers in health insurance. Most small-business owners don't have sufficient understanding of their responsibilities under the Affordable Care Act, which most people call Obamacare. *Entrepreneur* magazine reported on a study that found that out of 259 small-business owners surveyed by eHealth Inc., 56 percent misunderstood the employee mandate and didn't quite understand what their obligation was to carry it out.

The employee mandate is a section of the Affordable Care Act that requires that businesses with fifty or more full-time workers provide health insurance coverage for their employees. Under current law, if your business has more than fifty employees and you do not provide health insurance, you'll be required to pay an annual penalty of $2,000 per employee after thirty employees. If you have fewer than fifty employees, that health insurance mandate does not apply to your business.

Another area that's probably somewhat misunderstood has to do with the health insurance exchanges at the state levels. When they did this study, almost two-thirds of the people that responded said they didn't have any understanding of the exchanges, 20 percent said they had a fuzzy understanding of the exchanges, and only 18 percent said they could explain what an exchange was with some confidence.

The health insurance exchanges are state marketplaces where businesses and individuals can shop and compare plans. Most people are aware that the federal health-care exchange, which became available in October 2013, makes government-subsidized health insurance available for low-income individuals who are not getting coverage through their employer. But there's also something called the Small Business Health Options Program (SHOP) Marketplace, an exchange where small-business owners can pretty much do the same thing as the individuals and low-income folks.[18]

It was clear that most of those small-business owners in the survey were confused and frustrated about what their options were. When it comes time to make decisions for health-care benefits for your employees, you need to understand your responsibilities under the Affordable Care Act or have an advisor help with that. We make sure our clients are not on the hook for any penalties, but at the same time we also work closely with partner companies that specialize in health insurance so that we can provide appropriate benefits for our clients and their employees. Some clients will do best with the exchange, and we tell them that. If an exchange is not an appropriate place for them to go, we tell them where they can get better benefits for their employees and their families through insurance companies in whatever state they reside.

Your Personal CFO should assist you in reviewing your benefits: health, dental, vision, group disability, and group life. As to your retirement plan, the Personal CFO, in collaboration with your CPA and TPA, can recommend whether to do a defined contribution plan like a 401(k) or a profit-sharing plan or whether a defined-benefit plan is appropriate. Your Personal CFO and team would be working with you and collaborating with specialists like the TPA, who can run calculations on costs of the options available to you.

18 Catherine Clifford, "Small-Business Owners Still Confused About Health-Care Reform," *Entrepreneur*, March 21, 2013, https://www.entrepreneur.com/article/226174.

DR. SMITH'S SAFE HARBOR 401(K) AND PROFIT SHARING

Under a safe harbor 401(k) plan, an employer can match each eligible employee's contribution, dollar for dollar, up to 3 percent of the employee's compensation, and then the next 2 percent of pay can be matched at fifty cents on the dollar. Generally, "safe harbor" refers to the way the plan satisfies IRS rules for elective deferrals and employer matching. The IRS sets the maximum employee contribution each year, but let's say it's $18,000. Any employee, including the owner, can get that plus the match. So if you earn $100,000, you could contribute the $18,000, get a $4,000 match, and possibly add $6,000 as a result of a catch-up provision allowing higher contributions for those over age fifty who have not put enough away. That's up to $28,000 in retirement savings.

One client, Dr. Smith, who was under age fifty, wanted to increase his retirement savings, so he did a profit-sharing contribution. The TPA ran the calculations to determine the highest amount that he could put into a profit-sharing plan for himself and his employees and receive a deduction. He could put an additional $100,000 away on a deductible basis, but only $54,000 could go to him, including the 401(k) and the safe harbor match. So in his case, profit sharing with his employees allowed him to increase his retirement savings by $32,000 (that's $54,000 minus the $18,000 in the 401(k) and the $4,000 match).

Often the decision for the employer comes down to whether to pay the employees or pay the IRS. If, for example, the employer's combined state and federal marginal tax bracket is 50 percent and he could put $100,000 into tax-deductible retirement contributions, he'd save $50,000 in taxes. Let's say $50,000 of those contributions must go to his employees. He's going to save $50,000 in tax, but that

$50,000 is going to go to his employees. He gets to choose if he wants to give it to his employees or to the federal and state governments. The decision has to do with the business owners' desires—how tax sensitive they are. You would think most people don't want to pay any taxes or pay as little taxes as possible. I've had conversations with professionals and business owners who say, "I don't want to give my employees any more than I've already given them." I have others who say, "We want to do everything we can to help our employees." It's just a different mind-set for each company, whether it's a manufacturing company, a contractor, a dentist, a doctor, or an attorney. It can vary based on the owner's relationship with the employees, how long they stay, and what the turnover is.

A Personal CFO has to really understand the client's business. The profit-sharing plans have vesting schedules that are usually over a five-year time horizon. The longer-term employees will benefit from that. If an employee leaves early, they don't get to keep all the money that the employer put into the profit-sharing plan. Typically an employee may be vested 20 percent after the first year, 40 percent after the second, 60 percent after the third, 80 percent after the fourth, and 100 percent after the fifth year. An employee who leaves after two years would get 40 percent of the profit sharing, and the other 60 percent would stay in the plan. It's allocated for other expenses in the plan or future contributions.

To help set up such a plan, your Personal CFO will need to know the employees' job titles, their dates of birth, their incomes, and their dates of hire. All of that information goes into the formula the TPA uses to tell the employer, "This is how much you can put away to maximize your plan." Then the Personal CFO will collaborate on that decision with the CPA. The CPA says, "If you put this in, this is how much you're going to save in taxes." Now you're making an educated decision with knowledge of the pros and cons of your retirement plan contributions.

Each plan is a bit different based on what we're trying to accomplish for the employer.

Your Personal CFO will likely need to spend a lot of time with you to determine what will help you the most in making these decisions. But that's what a coach does. He encourages you. "Hey, I need to see you again. I'm coming to your office. We need to talk about this."

ONE CLIENT'S STORY

A couple, both attorneys, wanted to hire our firm to assist them in coordinating their financial and business lives. I take a limited number of clients on each year, but I was interested because Janet and James were in a unique situation and showed a true desire to experience the Power of a Plan. I was introduced to James by a university professor who also worked for the law firm James owned, among other business enterprises. James was in his fifties and had the drive to create a large financial legacy for his family and his community. I would call his law firm medium sized, but it had many attorneys across a variety of specialties.

Once we were hired, we held multiple meetings with them and went through our normal process of reaching out to their CPA and their attorney. That's when the story took an interesting turn. The couple's estate-planning attorney had been working in the main law firm for James for years, and yet his description of the business ownership didn't square with what James and Janet had told me. It's a little complicated, but basically James preferred not to have any ownership of a debt-collection agency, so he put it almost entirely in Janet's name, with 2 percent held by two others. Or at least he thought he did.

But when I discussed the debt-collection agency ownership with the couple's estate-planning attorney, we checked the documents and got a surprise. James had 50 percent ownership, which the attorney thought he needed to correct. There had been a gap in coordination in a fast-growing business. In the meantime, I passed this information along to his CPA, who was also fairly new to the team. We discussed the different ownership structures of the multiple companies James and Janet owned as part of figuring out how they might benefit from various tax strategies.

Once I had completed the comprehensive financial plan and business owner plan for them, I encouraged James to have a follow-up conversation with his CPA, as they needed to make some decisions regarding income-tax planning. James later informed me that he did have his follow-up conversation with his CPA and thanked me for reaching out to him. Thanks to discovering his common ownership of his profitable and unprofitable companies, he was able to use losses from one company to offset gains from the other, saving about $80,000 in income taxes.

"It sounds like you're experiencing the Power of a Plan," I told James. He laughed and said, "I absolutely am experiencing the Power of a Plan. If you want me to write that down, I'd be happy to do that." Well, James, thanks for sharing!

WORRY LESS, DREAM MORE

Business owners are often too busy to think about financial planning for themselves, their companies or professional practices, and their families. They may have a variety of experts advising them but need a holistic approach to bring that advice together into a plan that can evolve and adapt to their changing circumstances. That can only happen through a long-term relationship with a Personal CFO who offers this kind of comprehensive and collaborative approach.

The Power of a Plan is that it enables you to dream about your future and the legacy you'll leave and strive to accomplish your goals without worrying that you have not taken the steps needed to achieve them.

To recap some of the lessons I have learned in my years of working with clients:

- Just because someone is a Certified Financial Planner™, that doesn't mean they engage in the cross-disciplinary approach I have described throughout this book. In fact, most financial advisors won't routinely coordinate with your other professional advisors the way a Personal CFO does. I encourage you to find an advisor who believes in the Personal CFO concept.

- A potentially costly lack of coordination can occur even if you already have an excellent accountant, bookkeeper, lawyer, insurance agent, and other specialists on your team. If nobody but you is responsible for overseeing the entirety of your business and personal financial life, and you are too busy to do it comprehensively, you need a Personal CFO.

- Having a working spending plan is important whether you are behind in your bills or flush with money. Your cash management plan will show you the way to minimize the interest you pay on debt and maximize the earnings you get from your savings and investments.

- Managing the personal risks that significantly affect all of us, such as death and illness, is the foundation of financial planning and has to be dealt with before focusing on investing to gain wealth.

- Your investment and asset-allocation strategies should be determined not by your greed but by your need. The comprehensive financial-planning process you complete with your Personal CFO can help you understand your need.

- Real estate is like your other investments in that you should understand your objective in owning it. Your Personal CFO can help you make a strategy for owning the various types of real estate assets that are appropriate to your specific, personal needs.

- Retirement planning involves more than making sure your needs are met. It involves understanding what you find rewarding. Continuing to work, cutting back on work to spend time with family, and volunteering service to others are among people's different priorities. To accomplish these things, a Personal CFO can help you determine what it will take to become financially independent.

- Income taxes can create a tremendous drag on investment performance. But they don't have to if you make tax efficiency part of your financial planning. A Personal CFO can make sure you ask the right questions and coordinate between your investment advisor and CPA.

- If you haven't planned around estate taxes, you may be leaving more than you expect to the IRS and less of a legacy than you want for your family and community.

- Besides determining how your assets will be distributed to your heirs, you should be preparing them to receive the wealth that you have spent a lifetime creating, growing, preserving, and protecting. That preparation can begin in childhood.

- Anyone creating, buying, or selling a business should do some strategic planning for the continuity and succession issues that inevitably arise. These affect not only customers, clients, or patients but also key employees, partners, and family members.

When I am asked what I do for a living, my response is that we do planning for business owners and successful individuals who want to have a team of professionals collaborate on their behalf. Our role is to act like the client's Personal CFO.

My experience in doing comprehensive financial and business owner planning with clients has helped me to help them make better life decisions. These choices have positively affected their long-term and short-term goals while providing them a sense of security and a better understanding of where they are financially as it relates to their personal priorities.

When meeting with prospective clients, it is my objective to provide them with a valuable experience to better understand their situation and identify whether or not I believe that what we do will be of value to them. We take on only a select number of clients every year. Because of that, I want to make sure that there is a fit for me and for my clients in helping them to put their financial house in order. In the end, because of my educational and professional experience, I have a great deal of passion around the benefits that come from doing financial planning and business owner planning on a comprehensive basis.

After working with hundreds of individuals and business owners like you, we have found that you will benefit by working with an advisor who truly believes in the Personal CFO concept. If you have found this book helpful, I invite you to contact Stone Consulting Group and set up a consultation with one of our professionals so that you can also experience the Power of a Plan!

WHAT IS AN "ACCREDITED INVESTOR"?

Under the federal securities laws, a company or private fund may not offer or sell securities unless the transaction has been registered with the SEC or an exemption from registration is available. Certain securities offerings that are exempt from registration may only be offered to, or purchased by, persons who are *accredited investors*. One principal purpose of the accredited investor concept is to identify persons who can bear the economic risk of investing in these unregistered securities.

Unlike offerings registered with the SEC in which certain information is required to be disclosed, companies and private funds, such as a hedge fund or venture capital fund, engaging in these exempt offerings do not have to make prescribed disclosures to accredited investors. These offerings, sometimes referred to as *private placements*, involve unique risks, and you should be aware that you could lose your entire investment.

The SEC recently adopted rules to permit general advertising for certain exempt offerings.

ARE YOU AN ACCREDITED INVESTOR?

An *accredited investor*, in the context of a natural person, includes anyone who:

- earned income that exceeded $200,000 (or $300,000 together with a spouse) in each of the prior two years and reasonably expects the same for the current year,

or

- has a net worth over $1 million, either alone or together with a spouse (excluding the value of the person's primary residence).

On the income test, the person must satisfy the thresholds for the three years consistently either alone or with a spouse and cannot, for example, satisfy one year based on individual income and the next two years based on joint income with a spouse. The only exception is if a person is married within this period, in which case the person may satisfy the threshold on the basis of joint income for the years during which the person was married and on the basis of individual income for the other years.

In addition, entities such as banks, partnerships, corporations, nonprofits, and trusts may be accredited investors. Of the entities that would be considered accredited investors and depending on your circumstances, the following may be relevant to you:

- any trust with total assets in excess of $5 million, not formed to specifically purchase the subject securities, whose purchase is directed by a sophisticated person

or

- any entity in which all of the equity owners are accredited investors

In this context, a sophisticated person means the person must have, or the company or private fund offering the securities reasonably believes that this person has, sufficient knowledge and experience in financial and business matters to evaluate the merits and risks of the prospective investment.

Source: US Securities and Exchange Commission (SEC) Office of Investor Education and Advocacy

APPENDIX B

THE SERVE FIRST PHILOSOPHY

Since 1992, I have been affiliated with Lincoln Financial Advisors. They have a philosophy, "Serve First, Last and Always^SM", which I believe in and have reprinted here. It was written by legendary Lincoln financial advisor and manager Stuart Smith in the 1940s. In 2005, I received what's called the Stuart Smith Award from the Lincoln Financial Advisors Pacific Regional Planning Group. The award is given to the advisor in the Northern California, Oregon, Washington, Alaska, or Hawaii region whose business practices most closely represent the Serve First philosophy.

The Serve First philosophy means that we must approach our clients with all the human understanding possible and with only one desire: the desire to do the best job we can for that client.

We must help our clients to recognize both the problems and the opportunities they face and to accept the fact that we are the best people able to provide the financial counseling they require.

Our clients will react positively to sincere interest and genuine expertise the moment they recognize them. And they will spot insincerity and incompetence just as quickly.

To embody this philosophy through and through, we must first be fully committed in all that we do to "serve first, last and always." We must believe that there is no such thing as a client relationship out of which we must earn commissions in order to justify the work we have done.

Once we agree to work for our clients, once we commit to take the problems into our hands, we must believe that if we constantly deliver the very best service of which we are capable, without thought of pay when we do what is truly in the best interest of our client, our compensation, in the end, will always take care of itself.

To Strive in All My Personal Endeavors
To Serve **More** People **Better**

APPENDIX C

THE CREED

This client's financial affairs are a mess.

- His family suffers from this mess.

- It isn't their fault.

- They think they're in good shape.

- But someone strong will show them the light.

- I will be that person.

- I will inform them.

- I will focus on their problems.

- I will look them in the eye and quietly, gently, with dignity and singleness of purpose on their behalf, and with a respectful yet persistent manner, get them to put the problem into my hands.

I can be trusted with their confidence.

- I will uncover and identify the problems they face.

- I will work closely with them to correct mistakes they have made.

- Armed with logical reasoning and irrefutable facts, I will make every effort to persist, insist, and persuade, until they have put their financial affairs into the best possible order.

As a direct result of my efforts, this family will receive great value from my work and will benefit to the fullest degree from the financial resources they have accumulated during their lives.

As clients of mine, I owe them that.

* Source: Lincoln Financial Network

RESOURCES

PERSONAL SPENDING PLAN: UNDERSTANDING YOUR CASH FLOW

To better understand your cash flow, use the following personal spending plan to divide income and expenses into categories.

Client Name:		
INCOME:	**Monthly**	**Annually**
Salary - Client	$	$
Salary - Client #2	$	$
Bonuses	$	$
Self-Employment - Client	$	$
Self-Employment - Client #2	$	$
Social Security - Client	$	$
Social Security - Client #2	$	$
Rental Income	$	$
Pension	$	$
Investment Income	$	$
Annuity Income	$	$
Required Minimum Distributions	$	$
Other:	$	$
Other:	$	$
TOTAL INCOME:	**$**	**$**

EXPENSE SUMMARY:	MONTHLY	ANNUALLY
Housing	$	$
Transportation	$	$
Living Expenses	$	$
Discretionary	$	$
Taxes	$	$
Savings	$	$
Insurance	$	$
Debt	$	$
TOTAL:	**$**	**$**
SURPLUS / (DEFICIT)	**$**	**$**

DETAIL	MONTHLY	ANNUALLY
HOUSING:		
Rent/Mortgage	$	$
Homeowner's Insurance	$	$
Property Taxes	$	$
Maintenance/Repairs	$	$
Cleaning/Yard	$	$
UTILITIES:		
Electric/Gas	$	$
Cable TV/Satellite	$	$
Telephone/Cell	$	$
Water/Sewer	$	$
Garbage Collection	$	$
Other	$	$
TOTAL	**$**	**$**

TRANSPORTATION:		
Car Payments/Lease	$	$
Fuel	$	$
Car Insurance	$	$
Taxes/Registration/License	$	$
Repair/Maintenance	$	$
Other	$	$
TOTAL	**$**	**$**

LIVING EXPENSES:		
Groceries	$	$
Childcare	$	$
Child Support/Alimony	$	$
Clothing	$	$
Education	$	$
Medical/Dental	$	$
Other	$	$
TOTAL	**$**	**$**

DISCRETIONARY EXPENSES:		
Charity	$	$
Personal Care	$	$
Club Dues	$	$
Dining Out/Entertainment	$	$
Gifts	$	$
Pets	$	$
Recreation	$	$
Vacations	$	$
Professional Fees	$	$
Other	$	$
TOTAL	**$**	**$**

TAXES:		
Client Federal Taxes	$	$
Client #2 Federal Taxes	$	$
Client State Income Taxes	$	$
Client #2 State Income Taxes	$	$
Client FICA/Medicare	$	$
Client #2 FICA/Medicare	$	$
TOTAL	**$**	**$**

SAVINGS/INVESTING:		
Client Retirement Plan	$	$
Client #2 Retirement Plans	$	$
Other	$	$
Other	$	$
Educational	$	$
TOTAL	**$**	**$**

INSURANCE:		
Life-Client	$	$
Life-Client #2	$	$
Disability-Client	$	$
Disability-Client #2	$	$
Health/Dental/Vision	$	$
Long-Term Care-Client	$	$
Long-Term Care-Client #2	$	$
TOTAL	**$**	**$**

DEBT:		
Home Equity Loan	$	$
Credit Card Payments	$	$
Student Loans	$	$
Other Secured Loans	$	$
Other Unsecured Loans	$	$
TOTAL	**$**	**$**

TOTAL EXPENSES	**$**	**$**
SURPLUS/(DEFICIT)	**$**	**$**

WAIT-AND-SEE BUY-SELL AGREEMENT

The decision as to whether a cross purchase buy-sell agreement or a stock redemption plan is better may be difficult at the time it is drafted. Many business owners use the wait-and-see approach to defer this choice unitl after a death occurs.

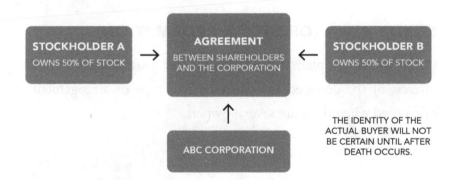

TYPICAL PLAN

- The corporation has the first option to purchase the stock at the price or formula set in the agreement.

- If the corporation fails to exercise its option, the surviving shareholders have a second option to purchase the stock.

- If they fail to purchase the stock, or only purchase a portion of it, then the corporation is required to purchase the remainder.

- If the insurance policies[19] are owned by and payable to the shareholders, the surviving shareholders may decide to lend the proceeds to the corporation after a death occurs, if they determine that a stock redemption would be most advantageous.

- When the corporation pays back the loan, it will not be ocnsidered income to the shareholder, except for interest which is paid on the loan.

- On the other hand, if a cross purchase plan is more advantageous the corporation will not exercise its first option to buy the stock.

ENTITY PLAN (OR STOCK REDEMPTION)

Under an entity plan the corporation (or partnership) buys the interest of the deceased (or partner). This type of arrangement is often used when there are several owners.

CORPORATION OR PARTNERSHIP — AGREEMENT WITH THE ENTITY — SHAREHOLDER #1 OR PARTNER #1 / SHAREHOLDER #2 OR PARTNER #2

---

19 Unless certain requirements are met, life insurance proceeds may be includable in income. See IRC Sec. 101(j).

CROSS-PURCHASE PLAN

Under this arrangement each surviving shareholder or parter agrees to buy the interest of any deceased business owner.

Source: Lincoln Financial Advisors: National Planning Department

ABOUT THE AUTHOR

David Stone is founder of Stone Consulting Group, an organization of financial professionals. Since 1992, David has offered financial planning services to professionals and business owners. His area of expertise is in designing and building a comprehensive financial plan that encompasses all the elements of his client's financial situation.

His clients' success comes not only from how well he understands financial strategy but in how well he knows his clients and their financial goals and objectives. David believes there is security in preparation and passes that on to his clients by helping them design a financial plan to create, preserve and protect their estate for their families.

David obtained his bachelor's in business management from Brigham Young University and an MBA from California State University, Sacramento. He is a CERTIFIED FINANCIAL PLANNER™ Professional (CFP®), Chartered Financial Consultant (ChFC®), Chartered Life Underwriter (CLU®), and Chartered Retirement Planning Counselor (CRPC®). He is a member of the Financial Planning Association and served on the board of directors for the Financial Planning Association of Northern California. David served as the Chairman of the Board of The Resource Group from 2015 –2016. The Resource Group is an invitation only group of the top 200 Financial Professionals inside of Lincoln Financial Advisors and Sagemark Consulting. David is also a BII Specialist with the Business Intelligence Institute.

David is a five-time recipient of Lincoln's Pacific Regional Planning Group (PRPG) Financial Planner of the Year Award, which encompasses California, Oregon, Washington, and Alaska. He received the PRPG Stuart Smith "Serve First" Award in 2006. Each year, one person who places the needs and interests of a client first and serves without regard to compensation is presented with this honor. David was recognized by the Invest in Others Charitable Foundation and earned Honorable Mention for the Lifetime Achievement Award in the 2016 Invest in Others Community Leadership Awards. Finally, Sacramento Magazine has listed David as a Five-Star Wealth Manager in 2011, 2012, 2013, 2014, 2015, and 2016.

Printed in the USA
CPSIA information can be obtained
at www.ICGtesting.com
JSHW012052140824
68134JS00035B/3385